Life Changing Self-Awareness

Acknowledgments

Special Thanks to our Family

Special thank to my loving wife of 31 years, Rosiland Y. Batten. Rosiland has been the backbone to my success and who has supported me unconditionally doing our marriage. I thank my five children who I love dearly, Kelvin R. Batten, Thomas L. Batten, Joshua T. Batten, Gerald L. Batten and my lovely daughter Alexis D. Batten. Also, thanks go to my father Theodore Batten Jr. and my late mother, Marie M. Batten, if not for them I would not be the person I am. We can not forget my two bothers Thomas Batten and my late brother Theodore Batten III.

Kelvin Batten—Co Author

I thank my loving mother Joy A. Pappas and father Richard G. Brown, who both has continuously inspired my life. Thanks also go to my sister Jennifer M. Brown, who supports my every endeavor.

Jeffrey A. Brown—Co Author

Three people deserve special mention

- **Program Director**—Charlotte Franklin *did a great job of pulling everything together for the book and keeping everything running smoothly.*

- **Copy Editor**—Kathleen Hines, RN *not only had the "eagle eyes" required of a copy editor (spotting stuff even missed by the tech editor), but punched up our prose to make it read better. Thanks, Kathleen!*

- **Project Editor**—Linda Reed *really made a difference, keeping everything straight, resolving any issues, and in general, just keeping everything on track. An experienced project editor like Linda can make all the difference between having a good experience as you go through final proofreading or suffering the horror of realizing that everything is mixed up. Believe me, I know.*

Life Changing Self-Awareness

Empowering Education and Career Growth

Kelvin Batten

Jeffrey A. Brown

iUniverse, Inc.

New York   Bloomington   Shanghai

Life Changing Self-Awareness
Empowering Education and Career Growth

iUniverse books may be ordered through booksellers or by contacting:

iUniverse
1663 Liberty Drive
Bloomington, IN 47403
www.iuniverse.com
1-800-Authors (1-800-288-4677)

Because of the dynamic nature of the Internet, any Web addresses or links contained in this book may have changed since publication and may no longer be valid.

The information, ideas, and suggestions in this book are not intended as a substitute for professional advice. Before following any suggestions contained in this book, you should consult your personal physician or mental health professional. Neither the author nor the publisher shall be liable or responsible for any loss or damage allegedly arising as a consequence of your use or application of any information or suggestions in this book.

ISBN: 978-0-595-47756-2

Printed in the United States of America

AUTHORS DISCLAIMER: The personal and career development resources in this book are not intended to be a substitute for therapy or professional advice. While all attempts have been made to verify information provided in this personal and career development publication, neither the personal and career development author nor the personal and career development publisher assumes any responsibility for errors, omissions or contrary interpretation of the personal and career development subject matter herein. There is no guarantee of validity of accuracy of any personal and career development content. Any perceived slight of specific people or organizations is unintentional.

The personal and career development contents are solely the opinion of the personal and career development author and should not be considered as a form of therapy, advice, direction and/or diagnosis or treatment of any kind: medical, spiritual, mental or other. If expert advice or counseling is needed, services of a competent professional should be sought. The personal and career development author and the personal and career development Publisher assume no responsibility or liability and specifically disclaim any warranty, express or implied for any personal and career development or otherwise products or personal and career development or otherwise services mentioned, or any personal and career development or otherwise techniques or practices described. The purchaser or reader of this personal and career development publication assumes responsibility for the use of these personal and career development materials and personal and career development articles and information. Neither the personal and career development author nor the personal and career development Publisher assumes any responsibility or liability whatsoever on the behalf of any purchaser or reader of these personal and career development materials.

Authors' Comments

Kelvin Batten and Jeffrey A. Brown are the co-authors of *Life Changing Self-Awareness*. These two successful entrepreneurs growing up as minorities in rough Virginia and Michigan neighborhoods, respectively, Kelvin and Jeffrey felt acutely uncertain about their chances of succeeding in life. However, their drive to survive got them through those formative years. Kelvin and Jeffrey would eventually use what they learned from their childhood challenges to improve not only their lives but the lives of many others.

Although their goal was to emphasize the positive aspects of Americans, Kelvin and Jeffrey occasionally ran into trouble with their viewers who perceived them as arrogant, condescending, and out of touch with the experiences of the average person. They both emphasize and support empowerment through education and career growth programs. As a result, the duo has received positive responses regarding this concept throughout different cities and educational communities. The primary goal for Kelvin and Jeffrey is to engage, enlighten and enhance the lives of people–without regard to age or ethnicity-through educational, job-readiness and self-esteem building programs that will prepare them for success.

Kelvin and Jeffrey teach, write, speak and coach individuals and companies about the skills necessary to become grounded in all human interactions while leveraging the advantages of life skills. They offer learning tools combined with a keen sense of humor to enhance and compliment each experience.

As CEO and COO, Kelvin and Jeffrey currently conduct seminars focusing on American business which include how to empower oneself in education and career growth, etiquette, effective speaking techniques, preparing executive resumes, preparing diverse people for corporate America, and others.

"*Life Changing Self-Awareness* empowering personal and career development book which **WILL MOTIVATE YOU** to take the steps needed to improve your life and help you to **ACHIEVE YOUR DREAMS**."

Kelvin Batten and Jeffrey A. Brown

Contents

Chapter 4 Your Life Changing Self Awareness Daily Self-Plan 139

Your Life Changing Self Awareness Daily Self-Plan 140

Introduction

The Life Changing Self Awareness book will teach people skills necessary for personal development and life independence growth. Further more this book is designed to help people in changing uncomfortable distress, as well as any unhealthy habits or behavior patterns in their life. It is also helpful in modifying, reducing, and eliminating concerns people might have and to start creating the life change they want. However, the book topics are just as necessary for basic life skills such as: self-esteem, behavior concerns, social skills, money management, health and much more. The book also includes how your supporters can help you when it is impossible for you to make rational decisions, take care of yourself, and keep yourself safe.

Life Changing Self Awareness concentrates on our youth and adults by addressing emotional, social and academic needs. We want to empower all to become self-sufficient through personal and career development training. In return it will assist our city in keeping our city streets clean and safe, improving quality of life and our communities. Our book will empower the reader how to become self-motivated and realize all of their individual potentialities. Additionally, it will assist you in becoming self supported by securing and maintain full-time employment.

Life Changing Self Awareness will assist in customizing a individual program designed by you, asking yourself a series of questions which will establish a "baseline" of emotions and actions which allows you to follow your own progress. This is through each person concentrating on our five concepts and your daily plan to address your life changing events, which could range from feeling good to out of control circumstances. Our techniques taught are chosen by each person for their usefulness which will vary from person to person. Our techniques are tailored to each person.

In order to be successful, each individual must spend at a minimal of fifteen to twenty minutes daily reviewing their individual program which has been designed especially for them. As you start becoming familiar with the element of your created individual program, the review time will shorten. Once the customized program is developed, keep a copy at hand for you to review daily when difficult situations arise. Don't forget to distribute copies to your supporters—which will be further discussed on page 142.

Overview of the Curriculum

Who can benefit from the Life Changing Self Awareness program?

This program can be used by anyone who has a set of circumstances that is interfering with their quality of life. This includes homelessness, child abuse and neglect, foster care, incarceration, substance abuse and chronic poverty. We will empower individuals to become self-sufficient through paid work and training. In return it will assist you in improving your quality of life in the community.

The Life Changing Self Awareness Concepts

- **Dreams, Hope, Goals (Fulfillment While Achieving Success)**
- **Self Esteem**
- **Personal Self Accountability & Responsibility**
- **Self-Advocacy**
- **Educating yourself on your circumstances**
- **Support Channels**

It can also be used to improve your life on an on going basis, preventing the onset of ineffective and troublesome behavior patterns, general poor health, chronic or acute.

Life Changing Self Awareness will assist in addressing or guiding your self independence from:

Re-entering society from the Department of Corrections	Attention Deficit Hyperactive Disorder—ADHD
Attention Deficit Disorder—ADD	Social Isolation
Department of Rehabilitation	Department of Human Services
Substance Addictions	Recovery from an Accident
Behavior Patterns	Unemployment
Depression	Adjustment to Retirement
Seasonal Affective Disorder	On-Going Medical Treatments
Chronic Overwork	Adjustment to Chronic Illness
Diabetes	Chronic Fatigue Syndrome
Seasonal Affective Disorder	Foster Care
Diabetes	Child Abuse
AND More…….	

The Life Changing Self Awareness Program is designed to assist you in:

➢ Monitoring life changing events through planned responses which utilize your Achievement Tools.

➢ Protecting yourself by having a plan of action with your supporters on your behalf, should you be incapable of handling a situation on your own.

➢ Staying in control of your situation or condition thus enjoying your life more. It is hard work, rewarding, emotional and "thinking" work.

➢ This program was designed not as an alteration of other programs and support given from other organizations, but a supplement to an ongoing self growth for independence. Additionally, we gathered useful information from people with a variety of life changing condition who want to work hard for independence and personal growth to enjoy life to its fullest.

The Life Changing Self Awareness Program Course Goals are to:

➢ Break the cycles of homelessness, incarceration, substance abuse and chronic poverty. We will empower individuals to become self-sufficient through paid work and training. In return it will assist our city in keeping our streets clean and safe, improving quality of life within our communities. To empower program participants, how to secure and maintain full-time employment, self-supported housing and sobriety.

➢ Establish a safety contract for all class members to freely participate and share their experience, comments or ask questions.

➢ Learn, understand and incorporate the overall Life Changing Self Awareness concept for self-sufficient and quality of life.

➢ Understanding the Life Changing Self Awareness Achievement Tools which are available and identify those, which will be most useful to you.

➢ Understand, through personal experience the concepts behind each of the Life Changing Self Awareness plans that are to be written and begin to create your own personal Achievement Tools while you incorporate them into your life.

Now you can move forward in your life one day at a time.

Life Changing Self Awareness Class Rules

1. Attendance is confidential & mandatory

2. All information shared in class is confidential

3. No criticism of others situations discussed

4. No judgments of others

5. No advice to others (we are not professionals)

6. Speak from your own experience

7. Listen to others—be open-minded and considerate

8. Be tolerant of emotional expression

9. Avoid dominating conversation

10. One person talks at a time—no secondary conversation

11. Speak without offending—listen without defending

12. Class interactions, discussions we all learn

13. Be on time to class by being aware of class schedules

Self-Awareness Personal Assessment (Part I)

_____

_____

_____

_____

_____

_____

_____

_____

_____

_____

_____

_____

_____

_____

_____

_____

_____

_____

_____

_____

_____

Chapter 1
Life Changing Self Awareness Concepts

Dreams, Hope, Goals
(Fulfillment While Achieving Success)

"Everyone should reach for Dreams, Hopes and Goals to make it reality"

➢ Dreams, Hopes & Goals can become reality if you work hard

➢ No matter what your life's circumstances are, always remember you are a full and complete Human Being

➢ You are a person first, not a condition, disease, or circumstances

➢ You are not lesser than others or "sub-human"

➢ Remember to leave your past in the past, it is not the present or the future

➢ You will grow and accomplish all of your Dreams, Hope and, Goals, if you put your mind to it.

➢ You can set your own goals and achieve them

➢ All of our experiences in life, have given us a different perspective on life

➢ Today begins the first day for self independence for your new quality of life

➢ Believe in yourself and use your good ideas to help decide what is important to you in life

Dreams, Hopes & Goals is one of our Achievement Tools

Self-Awareness Personal Assessment (Part II)

Building your Dreams, Hopes & Goals and begin working to make it reality.

If your life could be any way that you wanted;

1. What would it be like?

_____

_____

_____

_____

_____

2. Where would you live and/or who would you live with?

_____

_____

_____

_____

_____

3. What kind of your career and education will you have?

_____

_____

_____

_____

_____

4. What interests have you presently pursued?

_____

_____

_____

_____

_____

5. What other interests do you look forward to pursuing in the future?

_____

_____

_____

_____

_____

6. How do you plan to pursue these interests?

_____

_____

_____

_____

_____

7. What do you think is your expertise and/or what are you really good at?

_____

_____

_____

_____

_____

8. What skills are you planning or wanting to develop for the future?

_____

_____

_____

_____

_____

9. Do you plan to further your education and how?

_____

_____

_____

_____

_____

Self-Esteem
(Part I)

Self-esteem is simply the way we feel about ourselves.

Self-esteem is an integral part of personal happiness, fulfilling relationships and achievement.

> ➤ We exhibit low self-esteem when we feel a shame about our quality of life or feel that we cannot achieve our goals in life.

> ➤ We need to understand that we are no different than the next person. Just because everyone else is doing it, why should you

> ➤ Self-esteem can be raised or improved by believing in ourselves and who we are.

> ➤ There is a large component of positive self-esteem that comes from just being alive, and from being the wonderful, unique, special person of great value that you are.

> ➤ Using the Achievement Tools will improve your self-esteem.

Three Achievement Tools potentially having great positive influence in self-esteem are:

> ➤ Spirituality—the state, quality, manner, or fact of being concerned with or affecting the spirit or soul; "a spiritual approach to life"; "spiritual fulfillment"; "spiritual values"; "unearthly love".

> • Affirmation—asserting the existence or the truth of something or the act of affirming or asserting or stating something. Something declared to be true; a positive statement or judgment.

Learning to Love your Self and Love others will boost self esteem

---

Your self-esteem goal could be:

> ➤ Be around others that have the same beliefs as you.

> ➤ Spend less time focusing on ourselves.

> ➤ Spend more time improving ourselves or helping others.

This will happen if we are first satisfied and at peace with ourselves. If you love yourself, others will love you too.

Self-Esteem Exercise

Let's start building our self esteem and working to increase independence growth.

1. What can you do to increase your personal self esteem?

_____

_____

_____

_____

_____

_____

2. Do you believe in yourself?

_____

_____

_____

_____

_____

_____

3. Do you give yourself the credit you deserve?

_____

_____

_____

_____

_____

_____

Self-Esteem
(Part II)

Poor self-esteem leads to **bad choices** and **life decisions:**

- ➢ When we feel that no one likes us

- ➢ When we feel our hopes & dreams can not be accomplished

- ➢ When we are not able to make or keep friends

- ➢ When we are feeling we must depend on people, rather than being self-sufficient (Not depending on ourselves.

Our thoughts determine feelings—What are your thoughts?

- ➢ **Negative?** Low self-esteem-you deserve little

- ➢ **Positive?**   High self-esteem-you deserve a lot

Can you improve your thoughts? YES YOU CAN! How else can you raise self-esteem?

> ## Take control and be in charge of your life!

- ➢ Develop and apply your Achievement Tools (Particularly affirmations and spirituality).

- ➢ Find and study self-help books

- ➢ Reclaim and cultivate YOUR SENSE OF HUMOR

- ➢ Do things you enjoy and share them with others

- ➢ Utilize all forms of the Achievement Tools

- ➢ Consider available help of therapy or alternative therapy

- ➢ Use and practice cognitive therapy

- ➢ In with the positive thoughts; out with the negative thoughts

- ➢ Be your own best friend

Love and take care of yourself, | You deserve it!! |

Self-Esteem Exercise

1. Describe your present level of self-esteem and self-confidence:

    _____

    _____

    _____

    _____

    _____

    _____

2. In what ways has your daily life contributed to your present self-esteem?

    _____

    _____

    _____

    _____

    _____

3. If your self-esteem is low, what do you consider to be the main contributing factors?

    _____

    _____

    _____

    _____

    _____

    _____

4. List attributes you have to work on improving your self-esteem.

_____

_____

_____

_____

_____

_____

5. Circle each phrase or sentence below that applies to you.

Changing my thought processes	Believing in myself
Doing things I find scary or hard	Self-affirmation
Doing my best at all times	Lowering perfectionist standards
Focusing on the positive	Believing others who affirm my worth

Portioning myself off from the bad memories of the past

Knowing that the mood swings are not my fault

Knowing that stigma is no basis for shame

Knowing that I am the same as others

Accepting I may take longer than others to accomplish my goals or task

Thinking of myself as a good and positive person

Affirming "I think and act with self-confidence"

Measure and focus on my past successes

Giving myself credit for accomplishments

Determination to get more out of life

Self-acceptance   Self-discipline   Not getting upset over things

Living one day at a time

Realizing that I have not quit—that I've worked through my problems

6. What are other strategies you have developed to help raise your self-esteem and self-confidence?

_____

_____

_____

_____

_____

_____

7. List your most significant achievements, take your time and include everything. Remember, be honest with yourself.

_____

_____

_____

_____

_____

8. List attributes others see in you.

_____

_____

_____

_____

_____

9.   Circle the actions you should take to increase your self-esteem?

Develop a strong support system   Listen to others who affirm my worth

Work as a volunteer   Listen to friends, family

Pursue my career   Pursue hobbies and crafts

Do medication and relaxation exercises   Participate in community activities

Use creative expression (draw, paint write, dance, etc.)

Just keep getting out there and trying for the brass ring

Be goal-oriented   Practice consistently affirmative self-talk

Learn new skills   Listen to good music

Gardening   Be a good friend

Keep my house and room clean   Do work that I feel good doing

Write in a journal   Join special interest clubs

Take care of family, pets   Take care of me

Gain success in certain areas of my life

Exercise monitor and respond appropriately to my early warning signs

Look at why I am low or high and do something about it

Learn to relate to others more effectively and appropriately through self-help books, counseling, and work in my support channel.

Be around people I like and who like me-positive people who are sympathetic and uplifting.

Avoid people who bring me down   Giving myself credit when I succeed

Take small risks in a safe place, getting feedback from people who know me well

Keep cards, pictures of friends, and positive notes on bulletin boards where I will see them frequently

Have a special place to keep mementos and reminders of my achievements

Communicating With Diplomacy

Today we're going to look at the essentials of communicating effectively and how important it is in school, at home and in the workplace. We will be learning several different aspects of effective communication. Let's begin by getting you to give me the answer to a question that some of you may find difficult to answer. As you ponder this question, I want you to think about the last time that you were given unclear instructions regarding a project, task or even simple directions. Think about what happened. How did it make you feel?

Question: What do you think is the **single most important aspect** of communicating?

Answer:

_____

_____

_____

_____

_____

What gets in your way of being a good listener? Put a check in the box that applies to you.

◆ _____Listening filters—"Get to the point" filter. "Waiting to talk" filter.

◆ _____Physical filters—not giving your full attention. Thinking about what you're going to do when you get home.

◆ _____You hear what you want to hear.

◆ _____Personal bias

There are six keys to effective listening:

1. **L**ook at the speaker's delivery style, but don't make it your main focus.

2. **I**nsist on an overview. Use this when people seem to go on and on.

3. **S**ay the message back in your own words. Tells the person what you heard and understood. You can phrase it by saying, "If I'm hearing you correctly, you're saying".

4. **T**ake both mental and written notes if necessary.

5. **E**rase all preconceived ideas. Take a moment to consider before responding.

6. **N**ullify distractions—try to focus on what is being said.

Listening Exercise(s)

Let's see if you'll be able to put some of these key steps to practice. Listen to the following passage(s) and then be prepared to answer the questions that follow.

1) Bull Exercise

Procedure

In the space below draw a short vertical line to represent a mama bull, a papa bull, and a baby bull."

Solution/Discussion:

_____

_____

_____

_____

_____

Keep in mind that the first step to issuing instructions is to have a clear understanding of what you want.

2) Bus Exercise

Procedure

Answer the following problem: "You are driving a bus. You go east 12 miles, and turn south and go two miles and take on nine passengers, then you turn west and go three miles and let off four passengers. How old is the bus driver?

_____

_____

_____

Solution/Discussion:

_____

_____

_____

_____

_____

What do you think these exercises tell you about your listening skills?

_____

_____

_____

_____

How can you put into practice the six listening keys that we've discussed today?

_____

_____

_____

_____

Personality Styles

> **Fact: We listen and absorb ideas at a rate faster than people talk. On average, most talk at a rate of 125 words per minute, while we think at 400 to 500 worlds per minute. With this comparison, you could see how one's mind could tend to wander.**

There are four distinct personality styles that you should be aware of and if you're not careful, during your communication with them, you may step on their toes and they may stop listening to you. See if you can identify your own personality type as well as that of your employees with whom you deal with every day.

♦   **The Connector**—always wants to do a good job, gives lots of details when speaking, will be loyal and hardworking. His hot button is stability and he gets this through personal courtesies. If you must do any constructive criticism, give it privately. Notice their work and praise them.

♦   **The Networker**—has very high energy, goes in a million directions at once, sees the big picture but usually is poor at following through on details. His hot button is recognition and he gets this by being people oriented. Praise their work and do it publicly. Help this person unleash their creativity.

♦   **The Producer**—bottom-line oriented, hard working, abrupt and goal oriented. His hot button is power and he gets this through control. This person will thrive the more freedom you give them to implement things and take charge. If young, be aware that they might not have the maturity to realize when they have crossed the line with people in being too assertive. This person will get angry if you publicly criticize them. This person will love contests.

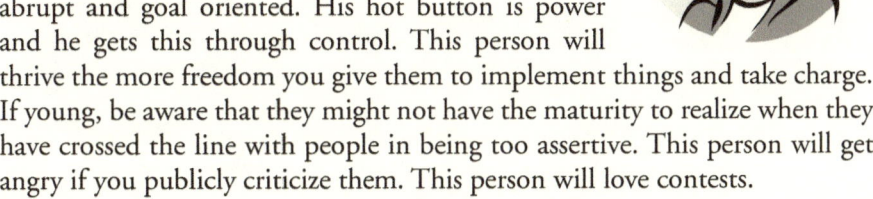

♦ **The Analyzer**—focused, organized, and precise. They believe you do things right or don't do them at all. His hot button is accuracy and he gets it through data. This person will do best with detailed instructions of what to do, when to do it and why they are doing it. They usually will not be big chatters with customers. Make sure you notice their precision and be patient with training them as they will want to know the "why" of everything you ask them to do.

Take into account the person's personality style and then try to speak from that perspective. Remember to always ask yourself, "How can I appeal to the lighter side of this issue and still make my point?" By knowing the four basic personality types, you allow yourself to creatively phrase things to get your intended audience to remain calm as opposed to get upset.

Also, remember that your message should be phrased so that it shatters barriers. What is meant by this? A good example of this was a hotel that was having problems with people stealing towels. Instead of putting up a sign saying, "Please don't take the towels." They made up a cute sign saying, "We are a little family hanging here for your use. Please don't take any of us out of this room, as we are very attached to each other. We do, however, have some cousins down in the gift shop that loves to travel. They would be happy to go home with you!" They said the number of towels being stolen virtually stopped and they had numerous customers asking if they could take a copy of the sign home with them.

The key lesson here: It's not what you say, but always how you say it!

Proverbs

3) Exercise: Proverbs

Procedure
   Try to figure out what the proverb is saying and
   record your answers in the spaces provided.

1) A period of preeminence is passed through by each and
   every canine.

_____

_____

_____

_____

_____

2) It is fruitless to become lachrymose because of scattered lacteal fluid.

_____

_____

_____

_____

3) Similar sire, similar scion.

_____

_____

_____

_____

_____

4)   Pulchritude does not penetrate the dermal plane.

_____

_____

_____

_____

_____

5)   It is not proper for mendicants to be indicative of preferences.

_____

_____

_____

_____

_____

6)   Your immature gallinaceans must not be calculated prior to their being produced.

_____

_____

_____

_____

_____

7)   It is fondness for notes of exchange that constitutes the tuberous structure of all satanically inspired principles.

_____

_____

_____

_____

Body Language and Nonverbal Cues

We have already determined that if we know our party's communication style, we can tailor our message to fit it. We have also determined that it's not what we say, but how we say it, which brings us to the discussion of body language and nonverbal cues and the roles that they play in the effective communication process. Body language displayed during normal conversation speaks volumes even if your mouth doesn't.

Nonverbal communication consists of gestures, body movements, posture, facial expressions, and eye contact. **Imagine a supervisor telling you that you're doing a great job with a big smile on his face and a relaxed body, you are probably going to believe them. On the other hand if your supervisor says to you, "you are doing a great job" and his teeth are gritted, he has a half smile and a stiff body, you will be confused as to what he really meant after he walks away.** What's wrong with this picture? How perceptive do you think the employee will be? Most likely you will feel that you are actually not working up to par, but you will not be sure why. Can you see the importance that body language and nonverbal cues have on your message?

Let's begin by completing the following exercise.

4) Exercise on Nonverbal Cues

Procedures

    a.   I will need volunteers to act/look like the emotion that I have on these index cards. The rest of the class will be asked to try and guess what the emotion is.

_____

_____

_____

_____

_____

Discussion

Hopefully, the thing that you have found you already know a vast majority of the nonverbal cues shown on the cards. Whether you realize it or not, you are already experts on reading nonverbal cues.

This exercise proves that you already know how to read some nonverbal cues. Believe it or not, only about 4% of the population understands how to ready body language. Think about the last messages you received from others that ticked you off. Was it really the words, tone of voice or the body language? By changing our voice tone on certain words or by adjusting our body language we can give a whole different meaning to what we said. Let's look at an example. Take the statement, "I did not tell her to come to the party." If you say:

"I did not tell her to come to the party"—phrase the statement so that it insinuates that someone else told her to come to the party, but you didn't tell her to come.

"I did not tell her to come to the party"—phrase the statement so that it insinuates that you may have suggested she not come, but you didn't tell her not to come.

"I did not tell her to come to the party"—phrase the statement so that it insinuates that you told her not to come to another event.

This example shows that depending on where you place the emphasis on a word, many different interpretations can be drawn. As managers and supervisors, it is imperative that you look at the body language you use and make sure it is congruent with your message. If you shift your eyes and look away, your people will not trust the message being given. If you raise your voice in a question while giving out quotas, it will sound as though you don't believe they are achievable. Reflect now on the messages you send every day to your employees and coworkers. Do you stand with your shoulders back, walk with confidence, make eye contact and smile? If you do, you will be seen as forceful and energetic; more of a leader. If you walk with your shoulders slumped, head down, speak in a flat tone, and/or fidget a lot, you will be seen as a person that can't make up their mind is more negative or that needs a lot of guidance. Remember, how you are perceived is up to you.

Fact: Research shows that only about 7% of feelings are expressed through words. Another 38% is expressed by the voice, rate of speech, etc., and 55% of feelings are conveyed through our eyes, face and gestures.

Six Body Language Signs to Watch For:

Resistance	
Interest	
Indifference	
Impatience	
Fear	
Puzzlement	

Instant Solution to the Most Common Communication Problems

1. **Remain objective**—*try to find out what the real issue is.*

2. **Listen**—*take notes if you have to*

3. **Ask questions**—*keep in mind that "why" puts people on the defensive. Substitute "why" for "what."*

4. **Concentrate on common ground**—*highlight the areas in which you agree.*

5. **Create common ground**—*your body language should match theirs; same as the tone and pitch.*

Written Communication

Written communication is just as important as oral communication. For the most part, the same guidelines should apply with a few simple do's and don'ts.

Do's:

- ➢ Facts only
- ➢ Timely
- ➢ Dates
- ➢ Places
- ➢ Witnesses
- ➢ Expectations
- ➢ Signatures

Don'ts:

- ➢ Assume
- ➢ Share
- ➢ Falsify
- ➢ Build a file
- ➢ Create a file

Other guidelines

- ➢ Put potentially harmful agreements in writing
- ➢ Keep your boss updated

Helpful Hints for E-mail

♦ Email should ALWAYS be considered public, not private. Do not write anything you would not want everyone in your office to see or that you do not want to have read back to you in a court of law.

♦ Never send e-mail when furious or exhausted. If possible, let it sit overnight or at least for a few hours. Then ask yourself what your response would be if you received such an email. Use that as your basis for editing it into a kinder and gentler document that makes the same point but in a less aggressive and hostile manner.

♦ When replying to a message, check the list of recipients. Be careful about hitting "Reply All." Do you want everyone to see your response?

♦ Be twice as diplomatic when using e-mail as you would in person. Spend the time to communicate with words that you would otherwise communicate with a smile or voice reflection. Try to frame critical e-mails in a positive way. Make positive comments before negative ones. Choose your words carefully.

♦ If you receive a personal or informal message, let the sender know if you are going to forward it before doing so. They may not want others to see it. By the same token, you never know to whom your e-mails may be forwarded.

♦ When you are blind copied on an e-mail realize and respect that this has been done for a reason and do not hit "Reply All." This can cause embarrassment for you and the sender.

Conflicts in the Communication's Process

We have looked at several different aspects of the communication's process. Hopefully by now we also realize the effects of body language, nonverbal cues, and the importance of being an active listener of the communications process. Let's take a look at communicating when there are conflicts involved. Often times we try to avoid conflict because we're afraid of the outcome or we're just unsure how the other person will take

us. However, if you learn how to communicate effectively, you'll be able to handle conflict without any problems. What types of conflict? Who knows? As a supervisor you may be put into the position of having to deal with a difficult employee or be the bearer of bad news. The key thing to remember in every situation is to **ALWAYS TELL THE TRUTH!**

1) **Be assertive.** Meaning, think about the situation before responding. Use key phrases like, "I see or I've noticed." Also, you must have respect for the other person. Use key phrases like "I respect that we may have different ideas about…" or "You know that I have the utmost respect for you, however…"
   ♦ **Deliver all bad news in private**—*do not humiliate.*
   ♦ **Begin the process informally**—*"We have to meet because of the project." Usually your employee will already know what you're talking about.*
   ♦ **Remain** objective

2) **Tell.** Meaning tell the other person what you think keeping in mind that you have your personal feelings (I feel) as well as your business feelings (I think).
   ♦ **Deliver in a positive manner**—*ask them what they think the punishment should be when appropriate.*
   ♦ **Add some praise**—*not only when you critique, but should be done often.*
   ♦ **Be specific**—*so not to confuse your employee*
   ♦ **Discuss the behavior only**—*not what you think about that behavior*

3) **Ask.** Meaning ask for change. Ask for what you would like to see or use phrases like, "Do you think we could try?"
   ♦ Be fair in your expectations
   ♦ Provide an opportunity for discussion.
   ♦ Listen
   ♦ Consider cultures

Fact: More than 85% of departing employees cite conflict as the cause for their departure and 75% of job stress is attributed to personal conflict. Between 1972 and 1992, employment lawsuits in the United States increased by 2200% Source: Alliance for Mediation and Conflict Resolution

How to Diffuse Emotion When Someone is Attacking You:

1. **Have Empathy:** Ask the person a series of specific questions designed to find out exactly what he or she means. Try to avoid being judgmental or defensive as you ask the questions. Try to see the world through the critic's eyes.

   By asking specific questions, you identify specific problems and demonstrate you are listening to the person and trying to see the situation as they see it. This helps to diffuse anger and hostility and introduces a problem-solving orientation in place of flaming or debating.

2. **Disarm the Critic:** Whether the critic is right or wrong, find some way to agree with him or her. What if the person attacking is making criticisms you think are unfair or not valid? You can agree in principle or find some grain of truth in the statement and agree with that, or acknowledge the person is understandably upset because of the way they view the situation. By not fighting back but finding a way to agree with your opponent, the person attacking runs out of ammunition and is successfully disarmed. Think of this as winning by avoiding a battle. As your critic calms down, he or she will be in a better mood to communicate.

   We all have a profound, almost irresistible tendency to defend ourselves when unjustly accused. If you give in to this tendency you will find the intensity of your opponent's attack increases. You will be adding bullets to their arsenal. If you respond with empathy and disarm their hostility, more often than not they will feel you are listening and respecting them.

3. **Feedback and Negotiation:** After listening to and disarming your critic, express your opinion with an acknowledgement that you might be wrong. Make the conflict based on fact rather than personality or pride. Avoid directing destructive labels at your critic. Do not try to make him feel stupid, worthless or inferior because of his error. If your critic continues to confront you, simply repeat your assertive response, politely but firmly over and over until the person tires out.

Sometimes the solution will have to be negotiated and compromised. You may have to settle for part of what you want. If you have conscientiously applied empathy and disarming techniques you will most likely get more of what you want. In some cases you will be wrong and the critic right. Your critic's respect for you will probably increase if you assertively agree with him or her, thank them for providing you with the information and apologize for any hurt, confusion, etc. you may have caused.

The crucial point is not whether or not you express your feelings, but the way you do it. If your message is, "I'm angry because you're criticizing me and you're no damn good," you will poison your relationship with that person. If you defend yourself from negative feedback in a defensive and vengeful way, you will reduce the prospect for productive interaction in the future. Your angry outburst may momentarily feel good; however, you may defeat yourself in the long run by burning your bridges.

If the shoe happens to be on the other foot and you are the person who has to criticize, you may find the following steps helpful.

1.   Identify the behavior you want to criticize. Direct your criticism at the action that you want changed, not at the person.

2.   Make criticisms specific. Do not say, "You always miss deadlines." Say, You missed the March 15th deadline for your report."

3.   Be sure the behavior you are criticizing can be changed. Foreign accents, for example, cannot always be changed.

4.   Use "I" and "we" to stress that you want to work out the problem together rather than making threats.

5.   Make sure the other person understands the reason for your criticism.

6.   Do not belabor the point.

7.   Offer incentives for changed behavior. Offer to help the person correct the problem.

8.   Do not set a tone of anger or sarcasm. Both are counterproductive.

9.   Show the person you understand his or her feelings.

10. If you are putting your criticism in writing, cool off before writing the critical letter or memo. Be sure only the person it is intended for sees it.

11. Begin by saying something good.

12. End by reaffirming your support and confidence in the person.

When you pull all these elements together, communicating will be a much easier concept. You can create a powerful force that teaches you to listen more intently and become more focused on your "customer." You should also challenge your teams to use their natural talents and the skills taught during this class to make communicating with ANYONE that they come in contact with a pleasurable experience.

Personal Self Accountability & Responsibility

Who is responsible for your independence and personal growth?

Is It:

➢ Your friends and family?

➢ Your teacher, doctor, neighbor or support channel?

➢ The state of Oklahoma?

NO!!!!!!

We are responsible for our own independence and personal growth. We alone must move past denial and self-pity, but we can use the above people for support if needed.

We are responsible for:

➢ Our own actions and consequences

➢ Our own physical fitness condition

➢ Our mental state of mind

➢ Our enjoyment and satisfaction from life

If you take responsibility for yourself, you will achieve the highest possible levels of enjoyment, satisfaction and quality of life as you move forward.

Reach and Achieve:

➢ Your Hopes

➢ Your Dreams

➢ Your Goals

➢ Your own Success

Self Responsibility is one of our Achievement Tools

Self-Advocacy

What is self-advocacy? Self help, support, and encouragement.

We become effective self-advocates when we:

> ➤ Believe in ourselves and understand we can accomplish our goals.
>
> ➤ Knowing our rights as a person and seeing that they are respected.
>
> ➤ Setting personal goal and working toward meeting them.

1. Getting the fact on our life and/or our life condition.
2. Planning our strategy.
3. Gathering support.
4. Targeting you efforts.
5. Being proactive—thinking and acting ahead.

We need to assert ourselves by expressing our need with:

- o Determination
- o Courage
- o Calmness
- o Persistence

Demand what you need and deserve!

Self-Advocacy is another Achievement Tool

Self-Advocacy Exercise

1. How have you learned what you know about yourself?

    _____

    _____

    _____

    _____

    _____

    _____

    _____

2. How can you learn more?

    _____

    _____

    _____

    _____

    _____

    _____

    _____

3. Do you feel that you take responsibility for yourself & your actions? How?

    _____

    _____

    _____

    _____

    _____

    _____

    _____

4. Why do you feel it is important to know all you can about yourself?

_____

_____

_____

_____

_____

_____

_____

5. In what ways do you plan to take more responsibility for yourself?

_____

_____

_____

_____

_____

_____

_____

Educate Yourself on Your Circumstances

We must educate our community, our past is not our future and you are part of main stream living.

We are all responsible for educating ourselves on:

➢ Our personal circumstances, physical and mental well being.

➢ Our trigger points prior to reacting to a situation

➢ Our treatments we are taking;

  o Doctor prescribed medications

  o Side effects of treatments and medications.

  o Therapies

  o Support Channels

➢ Our medical or support professionals

➢ Tools in our Achievement Toolbox that can and will help you.

➢ Options we have for independence in our life are:

  o Our Lifestyles

  o Our Living Space/Environment

  o Our Personal Relationships

  o Our Personal Activities

Sources for Education can come from:

➢ Workshops, lectures, and support groups

➢ Articles, books, newsletters, audiotapes, videotapes, internet and more

➢ Organizations related to your support need

➢ Medical professionals, persons with similar physical and mental circumstances

Education is an Achievement Tool!

Support Channels

Everyone needs support channels in their daily life. Remember you can count on your supporter, family, friends, support groups, and your medical professionals.

When your troubles become too much to handle, you should find someone to talk to. There are plenty of options out there. The right one is the one that makes you feel better after speaking with them about your concern.

What does a supporter do?

➤ Cares about and empathizes with your concern

➤ Affirms and validates your experiences

➤ Accepts you for who you are

➤ Listens to you and shares their experiences

➤ A person you can talk to about anything and be respected

➤ Is an advocate for you

➤ Enjoys being with you or around you

➤ Enjoys sharing fun activities with you

➤ Can help you in decision-making, sorting things out, and prioritizing concerns.

➤ Would be able to take over for you and keep you safe when you are not in control.

➤ Helps you to recognize improvements in yourself

Support is another tool in our Achievement Toolbox!

Support Channels Exercise

1. Do you feel alone and isolated?

_____

_____

_____

_____

_____

_____

2. Do you have a hard time reaching out?

_____

_____

_____

_____

_____

_____

3. What do you want from your supporter?

_____

_____

_____

_____

_____

_____

4. Do you attend support groups, if not why? Do you feel this could be a help to you?

_____

_____

_____

_____

_____

_____

5. Do you feel you have appropriate social skills?

_____

_____

_____

_____

_____

_____

6. List 5 people whom you can depend and trust to be part of your support channel?

_____

_____

_____

_____

_____

_____

Chapter 2
Conditions which can affect your quality of life

Personal Bill of Rights

1) I have the right to ask for what I want

2) I have the right to say no to requests or demands I can't meet.

3) I have the right to change my mind.

4) I have the right to make mistakes and to not be perfect.

5) I have the right to follow my own values and standards.

6) I have the right to express all of my feelings, both positive and negative, in a manner that will not hurt others.

7) I have the right to say no to anything when I feel I am not ready, it is not safe, or it violates my values.

8) I have the right to determine my own priorities.

9) I have the right not to be responsible for others behavior, actions, feelings or problems.

10) I have the right to expect honesty from others.

11) I have the right to feel angry at someone I love and to express this in a responsible manner.

12) I have the right to be uniquely myself.

13) I have the right to feel scared and say, "I'm afraid".

14) I have the right to say, "I don't know".

15) I have the right to make decisions based on my feelings, beliefs, and Values.

16) I have the right to my own reality.

17) I have the right not to give excuses or reasons for my behavior.

18) I have the right to my own needs for personal space and time.

19) I have the right to be playful and frivolous.

20) I have the right to be healthy.

21) I have the right to be in a non-abusive environment.

22) I have the right to change and grow.

23) I have the right to have my needs and wants respected by others.

24) I have the right to be treated with dignity and respect.

25) I have the right to grieve.

26) I have the right to a fulfilling sex life.

27) I have the right to be happy.

Stigma

What is stigma—a mark or characteristic indicative of a history of a disease or abnormality, a mark or token of infamy, disgrace, or reproach.

We can face stigma anywhere.

➢ In your classroom and school

➢ Within yourselves

➢ Our family, friends, and neighbors

➢ Our community, organization, and church

➢ Our employers and co-workers

➢ Our own support groups

➢ Our medical professionals

➢ While shopping in the mall

Eliminating stigma takes time and education because:

➢ Stigma is continually sent or broadcast on our televisions, the radio and society.

➢ We accept stigma as individuals whether it is blatant or subtle.

Stigmas are negative thoughts. We must change those negative thoughts in society to positive thoughts are an Achievement Tool within your grasp.

How can we repel stigma?

➢ Learn to set boundaries on what you accept.

➢ Let people know you accept your past, but it is not your future.

➢ We can gain the skill of not accepting the stigma put on you from society.

➢ Realize you have a future.

➢ You are a valuable person in society to everyone.

➢ Feel good about yourself.

➢ Stop allowing stigma to be a factor in our lives.

Warning Indicators

➤ Life Changing Self Awareness involves recognizing warning signs early enough to respond with action.

➤ What are your internal early warning indicators?

➤ What are your external warning indicators (Trigger Points)?

➤ How do your internal and external warning indicators relate to each other?

Our Life Style
Tools for Self Achievement
Current state of mine and physical being

↓

Improving our state of mine

LIFE CHANGING SELF AWARENESS TAKES SELF MOTIVATION

Avoid Destructive Behaviors

This lesson will provide information on the problems of drug use specific to health and working. The amount of drug education information that is available is extraordinary. Most people understand that drugs are bad, but do not always think about the consequences of drug use affecting their work. This lesson is not a substitute for substance abuse treatment. If a person is having difficulties related to the misuse of drugs, he or she should be referred to a trained substance abuse professional. This training is only designed as an educational program for job seekers. The drugs that will be discussed in this topic are alcohol, nicotine, caffeine, and illicit (marijuana, cocaine, heroine, LSD, etc.) drugs as whole group.

1. Begin the lesson by discussing drug tests at work. Inform students that employers have the right to test for illegal drug use. Use the following statistics published by the US Department of Labor that support the need for drug screening.

   - Seventy-one percent of illegal drug users are employed.

   - Of people who called a cocaine help line, 75 % indicated they used drugs while working, 64 % reported that drugs adversely affected their job performance, and 18 % had stolen from employers to support their drug habit.

   - Drug-using employees at GM average 40 sick days per year compared to 4.5 sick days for nonusers.

   - Employees who tested positive on a pre-employment screening at a Utah power company were five times more likely to be involved in a workplace

   - The insurance for Health Policy, out of Brandeis University, found that substance abuse is the number one health problem in the country.

   - Overall, substance abuse is estimated to cost U.S. Businesses more than $100 billion each year.

2. Discuss why substance abuse would cost employers so much money.

   • When workers miss work, they need to pay sick days and overtime for replacement workers.

   • Poor performance leads to work not getting done on time and poor quality. When products and services are not done correctly, they need to be done over; repeating any process and replacement of workers.

   • Workplace injuries cost companies a lot of money in prevention programs, worker's compensation, and replacement workers.

   • All of these factors lead to higher turnover. High turnover leads to money being spent on time & training new employees.

3. Discuss alcohol and illegal drug use. Use of alcohol or illegal drugs while working is definitely related to poor performance and accidents. Long-terms abuse of alcohol or illegal drugs is linked to health problems such as heart disease, cancer, and liver disease. Even occasional partying the night before work can impact a person's job & performance. Calling in sick and poor job performance when at work can affect a person's job evaluations and opportunities to advance in the company.

4. Discuss the use of cigarettes and working. All people should be aware about the health dangers of smoking. Nevertheless, students may not think about how smoking affects their job performance. According to information reported on the Smoke free Workplace News, www.smokefreekids.com/worknews.htm, smokers are absent 50 percent more often than nonsmoker and appear to be more unproductive due to frequent smoke breaks. Some evidence also suggests that smoking leads to decreased attentiveness and efficiency. Students should be informed that many companies are implementing strict workplace smoking policies. Is it unlikely that a person will be able to smoke whenever or wherever he or she wants on the job.

5. Discuss caffeine and working. There is no substantial link between caffeine use and health or work-related problems. Trainers may want to point out that too much caffeine can interfere with sleep. The person is tired due to lack of sleep and uses caffeine to stay awake and alert during the day. As mentioned previously, a good night's rest, a proper diet, and physical activity can lead to significant health benefits and energy. Remind students that caffeine is a stimulant and can cause nervousness and irritability. Although this may not hurt job performance, it certainly cannot help someone deal with the pressures of the job.

6. Discuss unprotected sex and sharing needles as behaviors associated with drug use that can have serious health consequences. Again, this type of information is available in great detail in many sources and most students probably have heard the information several times. Nevertheless, a reminder in the context of staying healthy would not hurt. Sharing needles when using drugs put a person at risk of being infected with many diseases, the most serious of which is the human immunodeficiency virus (HIV) that can lead to AIDS. Although having unprotected sex is not directly related to using drugs, a person's judgment is impaired under the influence of drugs or alcohol that can lead to making poor or risky decisions. Having unprotected sex and consequences will be covered more thoroughly in a following lesson title "Sexually Transmitted diseases."

If a person has a substance abuse problem, he or she will need professional help. People who exhibit addictive behaviors, such as smoking cigarettes, will probably need a greater incentive to stop than a lecture on the effect of smoking in the workplace. Hopefully, the students will consider the information presented and make appropriate life adjustments to improve their health and potential work performance.

Physical Fitness

> Any time a person changes his or her level of activity, risks are involved. This is especially true if a person has a physical disability such as a spinal cord injury or heart disease. It is important that trainers emphasize that students check with a physician before starting an exercise program.

A lesson on physical fitness should be fun. Most people know that being physically active is vital to good health. Nevertheless, using that knowledge is easier said that done; so, people need motivation. "Fitness" tends to conjure up images of five mile runs and hours in a weight room. Adopting a physically active lifestyle does not have to require much time or effort. This is especially true for people who are extremely sedentary. A slight increase in a person's activity level can lead to significant benefits. Instead of a "no pain, no gain" approach, this lesson will take an "every little bit helps" approach.

1. Discuss the benefits of fitness. Most people will know about losing weight, but other benefits are outlined below. It is important for people to realize that being physically fit and being thin are not always inclusive. A person who is thin but does not exercise may have low energy, clogged arteries, and trouble concentrating at work. On the other hand, a person with 10-20 pounds of extra fat can have a strong heart and excellent stamina at work due to regular exercise. However, it is important to keep in mind that a person who is overweight, regardless of his fitness level is at risk for health problems. The information below is based on an Internet article by John Abdo. The article is titled "The Benefits of Fitness," and it can be found at www.healthy.net.

   • Increasing fitness improves energy. People may disagree with this statement, especially after they start an exercise program and the yare sore, tired, and ready to quit. Inform the students that once they adopt a more physically active lifestyle, they will lose weight. Additionally, this increased energy transfer into being more productive at work and at home. It takes on 21 days to start a new habit.

   • Increasing fitness helps a person think well when under stress. Use the following information to explain this complex process. When we are under stress, our hearts beat faster, we may start to sweat, and we may breathe harder. If our bodies are not used to these changes, we tend to have a hard time thinking and handling the pressure. When we are physically active, the same changes in our bodies take place. If we are having fun and thinking while we are active, our bodies get practice for dealing with the increased heart rate, breathing, etc. Also, the more fit a person is, the more activity is needed to make these changes in the body. Therefore, when a person gets in a stressful situation, a fit body is not going to react as dramatically as an unfit body. An improved mind and ability to handle stress will definitely improve work performance.

- Increasing fitness improves muscles and bones. This benefit is obvious. For students who have jobs that require physical exertion, strong muscles and bones lead to improved performance and a decrease chance for injury.

- Increasing fitness improves the heart and lungs. If your heart and lungs are accustomed to physical activity, it is not going to seem like the end of the world when you need to go up a flight of stairs, walk more than a mile, or lift a few heavy boxes.

- Increased fitness improves your looks. As mentioned previously, improving your fitness may not lead to the body of a super model. However, toning muscles and losing fat may help a person drop a few inches around the waist and look healthier. This may give a person more confidence to continue engaging in exercise. People who are obese tend to feel uncomfortable when exercising, which leads to decreased motivation. Remember, every little bit helps.

2. Discuss ways a person can increase his physical activity. There are several things to consider when a person is planning to increase his activity level by starting an exercise program. A person will need to figure out where he will exercise, what equipment he might need, when he will exercise, and how to do the exercise appropriately. A health club would help answer these questions, but most students are not going to be able afford membership to a club. The information below should give some guidance for those who need and/or want to increase their activity levels.

- Before discussing some specific of exercise, review these principles of exercise outlined by Dale Bogle. The information is available at www.fitnesslink.com.

o **Progression**—start low and gradually increase. A person should consult a doctor before beginning.

o **Regularity**—try to exercise at least three times a week.

o **Overload**—to obtain the maximum benefit, you should exceed normal demands placed on the body, For example, if a person can walk a mile with little problem, she may have to walk fasters or longer.

o **Variety**—doing the same exercise day after day can ruin motivation. Try to spice things up.

o **Recovery**—Take a day off after targeting a group of muscles. This principle usually applies to running and lifting weights.

o **Balance**—make sure to include the 3 components of exercise below.

o **Specificity**—set goals and design exercise to meet these goals. If you want to run a 5K race, you should run instead of ride a bike.

- The first component of fitness is cardio respiratory. This is achieved through aerobic exercise. Aerobic exercise refers to exercise that keeps the heart beating at a higher rate than normal for an extended period of time (20-30 minutes). This is the easiest type of exercise because all that is really required is a good pair of shoes. Taking 30 minute walks three times a week is all that is needed to burn fat and lead to other health benefits. Other aerobic activities that require more equipment and/or a special place to do it include running, bike, aerobics, and swimming. Playing sports like tennis and basketball can also provide some aerobic benefits.

- The second component of fitness is strength and muscular endurance. A person who has more muscle is going to burn more calories. This means that adding muscle will help even when a person is lying down. Strength training usually requires weights. However, a person can do push-ups and sit-ups to obtain some of the benefits of weight training. There are many different types of exercise a person can do to increase strength. If there are students who are genuinely interested in starting a strength program, the person may want to contact a fitness trainer in the area to see if she would be willing to provide additional instruction. Alternatively, there may be classes offered through different communication agencies that a student could attend. There are also several fitness programs on television that can be taped.

- The final component of fitness is flexibility. Flexibility is achieved by doing basic stretching. Flexible muscles and joints are less likely to get injured while engaging in physical activity. There are several types of flexibility exercises, and they often are part of aerobics or strength training. Use similar resources mentioned with strength training to teach specific flexibility exercises.

3. The information in number 2 dealt specifically with exercise programs, but there are many ways a person can become more active without engaging in a fitness program which don't cost any money. Ask the students if they can think of any.

   o Use stairs instead of the elevator.

   o Park in a place that requires you to walk farther.

   o Walk or ride a bike to work.

   o Walk to the next bus stop.

   o Go window shopping (but do not stop to look very long).

   o Take your dog for a walk.

   o Use your 15 minute break at work to go for a walk.

   o Do a few push-ups or sit-ups during commercials.

   o Housework and yard work burn calories.

As everyone does, we need a complete physical examination at least once a year or more often if physical and mental indicators increase significantly.

There are many physical problems that themselves cause symptoms similar to psychiatric symptoms—among them:

➤ Hyperglycemia (Diabetes)

➤ Some chronic physical diseases such as angina, arthritis, asthma or diabetes

➤ Head injuries

➢ Hormonal imbalance

➢ Medication side effects

➢ Allergies to food, molds, vapors, medicine

➢ Exposure to poisons (mercury, lead, etc.)

➢ Lack of adequate lights in darker months—this is known as the "Seasonal affect disorder" better known as "SAD"

➢ Surviving Peer Pressure

➢ ADD or ADHD

Adults and youth should start and maintain an exercise program. Students engage in activities that help them to be more physically active.

Physical Fitness Exercise

1. Do you have any medical problems or diseases?

_____

_____

2. What are they?

_____

_____

3. Do you take any medications for these problems or have a special diet? If so, what are they?

_____

_____

_____

_____

_____

_____

Physical Examination
Seek and Follow Appropriate Medical Advice

This lesson will cover a broad range of topics to provide the student with information about maximizing health-care services. Going to see a doctor is not going to guarantee that a person will get well. You need to know what to ask and follow the directions the doctor gives you. Additionally, you need to be able to pay for these services. It is almost impossible to pay for good healthcare out-of-pocket. This is the purpose for the discussion on health insurance.

1. Discuss the importance of seeking medical care when needed. Many people do not go to the doctor because of inconvenience, money and fear. These are all legitimate reasons for avoiding a doctor's office. However, stress to students that putting off seeing a doctor can cause greater inconvenience, money and fear.

2. Discuss available health-care options in your community. In general, if a person has health insurance through a job or the government (Medicaid), he will be given a list of what physicians he can see. Most insurance companies require that people see an OR(PCP) primary care physician before going to a specialist. Inform students that they can go see a specialist any time they want, but they will most likely have to pay for the visit themselves. As a class, go through the Yellow Pages and look up different types of health care providers. The best section to look under is "Physicians." This will give a list of physicians by specialty. Most people will go to an internal medicine physician or family practice physician for basic health care such as colds, sprains, cuts, etc. Again people who have health insurance would pick their doctor from a list that the insurance companies provided. Have the students pick out other specialists and discuss what problems those physicians treat. For example, a dermatologist deals with skin problems, an orthopedist treats injuries to bones, joints and muscles, and an ophthalmologist treats problems with eyes.

3. Discuss various health-care options available in your community. Of course, the clinic where your doctor is located is where you go for basic medical care. Insurance companies usually dictate where a person can go for emergency hospital care. Have students look through the Yellow Pages to identify different hospitals and clinics in the area. Discuss whether there is free medical care available in the community and where it is located. Discuss alternative forms of medical care such as chiropractic

therapy, massage therapy, and acupuncture. These are alternative ways to relieve pain and discomfort especially in the back.

4. Discuss how to get health insurance. Most people get health insurance through their employer. People who are disabled or retired are entitled to government health insurance through the Medicaid and Medicare systems. A person who is not eligible for health insurance from any of these sources can purchase health insurance independently through an insurance company. However, the monthly premiums (amount of money the person pays for the insurance) are expensive, and coverage is limited. When health insurance is offered through work, the company usually pays part of the premium and the employee pays the rest each month. This will entitle the employee and family, if covered, to seek medical treatment at a significantly reduced cost. Depending on the coverage, the employee may have to pay certain percentage of the total medical costs, a flat fee for each visit to the doctor, or may pay nothing at all. The amount a person pays toward the premium and the amount of coverage a person gets is going to very tremendously. Common areas in which insurance companies pay most of the cost include: doctor visits, routine diagnostic services (x-ray, blood and urine tests), medical treatment, approved medications, emergency services, and hospital costs.

5. When a person goes to a doctor, they have the right to have all medical decisions explained to them. Some doctors do a good job at communicating with patients and some doctors do a poor job. The patient also has a responsibility to explain all health problems and answers to all questions from the doctor honestly. The following is a list of information a person should ask a doctor during a doctor's visit.

- Anytime you do not understand something the doctor says, ask her to explain it to you in layman terms.

- When a doctor indicates that she wants to perform a diagnostic test beyond standard measurements such as weight, blood pressure, and temperature, you can ask what she is looking for when doing an x-ray, blood test, or any other tests.

- You should ask when to expect the results and an explanation of all diagnostic tests.

- When a doctor gives you a diagnosis, but you do not understand what it means, you can ask the doctor to explain it to you.

- When a doctor tells you to do something to help an ailment, such apply ice to a sprained ankle, you can ask the doctor how that will help.

- Anytime the doctor gives you an instruction and you do not understand it or need further clarification, ask him to provide more information.

- Anytime a doctor prescribes medications, you can ask: Why? For how long? What are the side effects? The pharmacist can also answer these questions.

- Before you leave the doctor's office you should make sure you know whether you need to call the doctor for any test results or need to schedule a follow-up visit.

6. Discuss the importance of following directions for taking medications exactly as written on the label or handout provided. Taking the wrong amount at the wrong time along with certain food or drugs can make the medications completely ineffective. A worst-case scenario of not following the directions is illness or death. The Food and Drug Administration provides the following tips for taking medications safely.

   - If your symptoms are not improving, call you doctor. You may need a different dosage or drug. Alternatively, the drug may need to be in your system for a while before improvements are noticed.

   - If you get any severe side affects, call you doctor. Examples include vomiting, trouble breathing, headaches, rashes, and loss of consciousness

   - Make a list of medications you are on and a list of all your allergies..

   - Do not stop taking medications when you feel better. Follow the advice about when you should stop.

   - Check drug labels for specific instructions such as 'take with food" or "do not take with milk."

   - Check to see where the medications should be stored.

   - Always keep medications out of the reach of children.

   - Never let another person take your medications and never take the medication of another person. Even though your symptoms may be the same, you may be suffering from an entirely different illness.

- Keep a list of all drugs you are taking, so your doctor and pharmacist can make appropriate decisions about which medications would be safe.

7. Pass around the different drug labels and have students read the instructions out loud. Assist students who have difficulty reading. Ask the students questions to test their understanding of the instructions. Use the following examples as guides for the questioning.

- The instructions indicate that a person should take no more that eight pills in a 24 hour period (two every six hours). It is OK to take three pills every five hours?

- The instructions indicate that the medication should not be mixed with alcohol. It is OK to take the medication and have two beers at dinner?

- The instructions indicate that a person should not operate heavy machinery when taking the medication. It is OK to drive?

- The instructions indicate that the pills should be taken with food. It is OK to take the medications and then eat something an hour later?

- The instructions indicate to take the medications until al the pills are gone. It is OK to stop a few days earlier if you are feeling better?

Bring with you to the physical examination:

➢ Your medical history and that of your family, including all major illnesses and surgeries.

➢ A list of all your medications, vitamins, minerals, and healthcare preparations with dosage, reason for taking, and length of time taken.

Report changes in:

Appetite	Thinking patterns
Anxiety	Weight
Sleep patterns	Concentration
Diet	Sexual interest
Nervousness	Loss of interest in pleasurable things

Also report:

Headaches	Loss of balance
Periods of amnesia	Vision problems
Nausea or diarrhea	Fainting or dizziness
Double vision	Coordination changes
Weakness in arms or legs	Seizures
Numbness or tingling anywhere	Fever stressful life events
Any other unusual symptoms	

Adults and Students are able to make appropriate decisions about health care services when needed. When students become ill, they increase their likelihood of getting better because they communicate with their physician and follow instructions carefully.

Physical Examination Exercise

1. List all medications, vitamins, and health care preparations you are using.

Medication	Dosage	Usage

2. Medical history—Surgery, diseases, conditions, etc.

    a. Yourself

_____

_____

_____

_____

_____

_____

    b. Mother's side of the family

_____

_____

_____

_____

_____

c. Father's side of the family

_____

_____

_____

_____

_____

_____

3. Describe changes in:

Appetite or diet

_____

_____

Weight

_____

_____

Sleep patterns

_____

_____

Sexual interest

_____

_____

Ability to concentrate

_____

_____

Memory

_____

_____

Bowel and urinary habits

_____

_____

4. If you have recently had any of the following symptoms, describe them:

Headaches

_____

_____

Numbness or tingling (where?)

_____

_____

Double vision or vision problems

_____

_____

Mood swings

_____

_____

Weakness in arms or legs

_____

_____

Fever

_____

_____

Nausea, diarrhea, or vomiting

_____

_____

Fainting or dizziness

_____

_____

Seizures

_____

_____

5.   Describe your diet

_____

_____

_____

_____

_____

6. Describe your use of caffeine-containing substances (coffee, tea, chocolate, soft drinks):

_____

_____

_____

_____

_____

_____

Describe your use of alcohol;

_____

_____

_____

_____

_____

_____

7. Describe your smoking habits:

_____

_____

_____

_____

_____

_____

Doctors Question Form

You may find the following format useful. Keep these sheets in your health care file for easy reference.

Question

_____

_____

_____

_____

_____

_____

Response

_____

_____

_____

_____

_____

Action I need to take because of information from my physician:

_____

_____

_____

_____

Tips for Finding Good Health Care Professionals

➢ Educate yourself

➢ Ask health care organizations, friends, and current health care professionals for referrals.

➢ Interview professionals who might meet your needs before making long term commitments.

➢ Explore a variety of approaches, including safe, non-invasive alternatives

This is a very personal task—don't get talked into working with someone you are not comfortable with

Your team of health care professionals might include:

Medical Doctors	Allergists
Counselors	Chiropractors
Psychiatrists	Pharmacists
Social workers	Nationalists
Endocrinologists	Therapists
Osteopaths	Naturopaths
Homeopathic physicians	Occupational or massage therapists

Cost and health care plans can be limiting factors. We need to work together for health care reform. Use your right to vote.

Exercise

1. Whom do you want to include on your health care team? Circle those that apply to you.

Medical doctors	Psychiatrists	Pharmacists
Endocrinologists	Allergists	Osteopaths
Therapists or counselors	Social workers	Art therapies
Chiropractors	Body workers	Homeopathic physicians
Nutritional therapist	Occupational therapist	
Massage therapist	Psycho pharmacologists	

2. What attributes do you want from the health professionals on your team?

_____

_____

_____

_____

_____

_____

3. What are some unwanted attributes of health care professionals.

_____   _____

_____   _____

_____   _____

_____   _____

_____   _____

_____   _____

4. What other qualities in health care professionals do you want to avoid?

_____

_____

_____

_____

_____

_____

5. Describe your ideal treatment scenario:

_____

_____

_____

_____

_____

_____

Attention Deficit Hyperactive Disorder—ADHD

What is ADHD?

➢ Attention Deficit Hyperactivity Disorder (ADHD) is a condition that becomes apparent in some individuals in the preschool and early school years. It is hard for these individual to control their behavior and/or pay attention. It is estimated that between 3 and 5 percent of individuals have ADHD, or approximately 2 million individuals in the United States. This means that in a classroom of 25 to 30 individuals, it is likely that at least one will have ADHD.

➢ A child with ADHD faces a difficult but not insurmountable task ahead. In order to achieve his or her full potential, he or she should receive help, guidance, and understanding from parents, guidance counselors, and the public education system.

➢ ADHD often continues into adulthood.

What are ADHD Symptoms

The principal characteristics of ADHD are **inattention**, **hyperactivity**, and **impulsivity**. These symptoms appear early in a child's life. Because many normal individual may have these symptoms, but at a low level, or the symptoms may be caused by another disorder, it is important that the child receive a thorough examination and appropriate diagnosis by a well-qualified professional.

Symptoms of ADHD will appear over the course of many months, often with the symptoms of impulsiveness and hyperactivity preceding those of inattention, which may not emerge for a year or more. Different symptoms may appear in different settings, depending on the demands the situation may pose for the child's self-control. A child who "can't sit still" or is otherwise disruptive will be noticeable in school, but the inattentive daydreamer may be overlooked. The impulsive child who acts before thinking may be considered a "discipline problem," while the child who is passive or sluggish may be viewed as merely unmotivated. Yet both may have different types of ADHD. All individuals are sometimes restless, sometimes act without thinking, and sometimes daydream their time away. When the child's hyperactivity, distractibility, poor concentration, or impulsivity begin to affect performance in school, social relationships with other individual, or behavior at home, ADHD may be suspected but because the symptoms vary so much across settings, ADHD is not easy to diagnose. This is especially true when inattentiveness is the primary symptom.

What is Hyperactivity-Impulsivity

Hyperactive individuals always seem to be "on the go" or constantly in motion. They dash around touching or playing with whatever is in sight, or talk incessantly. Sitting still at dinner or during a school lesson or story can be a difficult task. They squirm and fidget in their seats or roam around the room. Or they may wiggle their feet, touch everything, or noisily tap their pencil. Hyperactive teenagers or adults may feel internally restless. They often report needing to stay busy and may try to do several things at once.

Impulsive individuals seem unable to curb their immediate reactions or think before they act. They will often blurt out inappropriate comments, display their emotions without restraint, and act without regard for the later consequences of their conduct. Their impulsivity may make it hard for them to wait for things they want or to take their turn in games. They may grab a toy from another child or hit when they're upset. Even as teenagers or adults, they impulsively choose to do things that have an immediate but small payoff rather than engage in activities that may take more effort yet provide much greater but delayed rewards.

Some signs of Hyperactivity-Impulsivity are:

➢ Feeling restless, often fidgeting with hands or feet, or squirming while seated
➢ Running, climbing, or leaving a seat in situations where sitting or quiet behavior is expected
➢ Blurting out answers before hearing the whole question
➢ Having difficulty waiting in line or taking turns.

What is Inattention

➢ Individuals who are inattentive have a hard time keeping their minds on any one thing and may get bored with a task after only a few minutes. If they are doing something they really enjoy, they have no trouble paying attention. But focusing deliberately, conscious attention to organizing and completing a task or even learning something new is difficult.

➢ Homework is particularly hard for these individuals. They will forget to write down an assignment, or leave it at school. They will forget to bring a book home, or bring the wrong one. The homework, if finally finished, is full of errors and erasures. Homework is often accompanied by frustration for both parent and child.

The signs of inattention:

> ➤ Often becoming easily distracted by irrelevant sights and sounds

> ➤ Often failing to pay attention to details and making careless mistakes

> ➤ Rarely following instructions carefully and completely losing or forgetting things like toys, or pencils, books and tools needed for a task

> ➤ Often skipping from one uncompleted activity to another.

Individual diagnosed with the Predominantly Inattentive Type of ADHD are seldom impulsive or hyperactive, yet they have significant problems paying attention. They appear to be daydreaming, "spacey," easily confused, slow moving, and lethargic. They may have difficulty processing information as quickly and accurately as other individual.

When the teacher gives oral or even written instructions, this child has a hard time understanding what he or she is supposed to do and makes frequent mistakes. Yet the child may sit quietly, unobtrusively, and even appear to be working but not fully attending to or understanding the task and the instructions.

These individual don't show significant problems with impulsivity and over activity in the classroom, on the play ground or at home. They may get along better with other individuals than the more impulsive and hyperactive types of ADHD, and they may not have the same sort of social problems common with the combined type of ADHD. So often their problems with inattention are overlooked. But they need help just as much as individuals with other types of ADHD, who cause more obvious problems in the classroom.

Diagnosis

Some parents see signs of inattention, hyperactivity, and impulsivity in their toddler long before the child enters school. The child may lose interest in playing a game or watching a TV show, or may run around completely out of control. But because individuals mature at different rates and are very different in personality, temperament, and energy levels, it's useful to get an expert's opinion on whether the behavior is appropriate for the child's age. Parents can ask their child's pediatrician, or a child psychologist or psychiatrist, to assess whether their toddler has an attention deficit hyperactivity disorder.

ADHD may be suspected by a parent or caretaker or may go unnoticed until the child runs into problems at school. Given that ADHD tends to affect functions most strongly in school, sometimes the teacher is the first to recognize that a child is hyperactive or inattentive and may point it out to the parents and/or consult with the school psychologist. Because teachers work with many individuals, they come to know how "average" individuals behave in learning situations that require attention and self-control. However, teachers sometimes fail to notice the needs of individual who may be more inattentive and passive yet who are quiet and cooperative, such as those with the predominantly inattentive form of ADHD.

Professionals Who Make the Diagnosis.

If ADHD is suspected, to whom can the family turn? What kinds of specialists do they need?

Ideally, the diagnosis should be made by a professional in your area with training in ADHD or in the diagnosis of mental disorders. Child psychiatrists and psychologists, developmental/behavioral pediatricians, or behavioral neurologists are those most often trained in differential diagnosis. Clinical social workers may also have such training.

The family can start by talking with the child's pediatrician or their family doctor. Some pediatricians may do the assessment themselves, but often they refer the family to an appropriate mental health specialist they know and trust. In addition, state and local agencies that serve families and individuals, as well as some of the volunteer organizations listed at the end of this document, can help identify appropriate specialists.

Specialty	Can Diagnose ADHD	Can prescribe medication, if needed	Provides counseling or training
Psychiatrists	Yes	Yes	yes
Psychologists	Yes	Yes	yes
Pediatricians or Family Physicians	Yes	Yes	no
Neurologists	Yes	Yes	no
Clinical Social workers	Yes	No	yes

What Causes ADHD?

1. One of the first questions a parent will have is "Why? What went wrong?" "Did I do something to cause this?" There is little compelling evidence at this time that ADHD can arise purely from social factors or child-rearing methods. Most substantiated causes appear to fall in the realm of neurobiology and genetics. This is not to say that environmental factors may not influence the severity of the disorder, and especially the degree of impairment and suffering the child may experience, but that such factors do not seem to give rise to the condition by themselves.

2. The parents' focus should be on looking forward and finding the best possible way to help their child. Scientists are studying causes in an effort to identify better ways to treat, and perhaps someday, to prevent ADHD. They are finding more and more evidence that ADHD does not stem from the home environment, but from biological causes. Knowing this can remove a huge burden of guilt from parents who might blame themselves for their child's behavior.

Disorders that Sometimes Accompany ADHD

➢ **Learning Disabilities**—Many individuals with ADHD—approximately 20 to 30 percent—also have a specific learning disabilities (LD). These disabilities include difficulty in understanding certain sounds or words and/or difficulty in expressing oneself in words. In school age individuals, reading or spelling disabilities, writing disorders, and arithmetic disorders may appear. A type of reading disorder, dyslexia, is quite widespread. Reading disabilities affect up to 8 percent of elementary school individual.

➢ **Tourettes Syndrome**—A very small proportion of people with ADHD have a neurological disorder called Tourettes syndrome. People with Tourettes syndrome have various nervous tics and repetitive mannerisms, such as eye blinks, facial twitches, or grimacing. Others may clear their throats frequently, snort, sniff, or bark out words. These behaviors can be controlled with medication. While very few individuals have this syndrome, many of the cases of Tourettes syndrome have associated ADHD. In such cases, both disorders often require treatment that may include medications.

➢ **Anxiety and Depression**—Some individuals with ADHD often have co-occurring anxiety or depression. If the anxiety or depression is recognized and treated, the child will be better able to handle the problems that accompany ADHD. Conversely, effective treatment of ADHD can have a positive impact on anxiety as the child is better able to master academic tasks.

Which Treatment Should My Child Have?

For individuals with ADHD, no single treatment is the answer for every child. A child may sometimes have undesirable side effects to a medication that would make that particular treatment unacceptable. If a child with ADHD also has anxiety or depression, a treatment combining medication and behavioral therapy might be best. Each child's needs and personal history must be carefully considered.

➢ **Medications**—For decades, medications have been used to treat the symptoms of ADHD.

The medications that seem to be the most effective are a class of drugs known as stimulants. Following is a list of the stimulants, their trade (or brand) names, and their generic names. "Approved age" means that the drug has been tested and found safe and effective in individual of that age.

Trade Name	Generic Name	Approved Age
Adderall	Amphetamine	3 and older
Concerta	Methylphenidate (long acting)	6 and older
Cylert*	Pemoline	6 and older
Dexedrine	Dextroamphetamine	3 and older
Dextrostat	Dextroamphetamine	3 and older
Focalin	Dexmethylphenidate	6 and older
Metadate ER	Methylphenidate (extended release)	6 and older
Metadate CD	Methylphenidate (extended release)	6 and older
Ritalin	Methylphenidate	6 and older
Ritalin SR	Methylphenidate (extended release)	6 and older
Ritalin LA	Methylphenidate (long acting)	6 and older

> Because of its potential for serious side effects affecting the liver, Cylert should not ordinarily be considered as first-line drug therapy for ADHD.

The Family and the ADHD Child

➢ Medication can help the ADHD child in everyday life.

➢ Better able to control some of the behavior problems that have led to trouble with parents and siblings. But it takes time to undo the frustration, blame, and anger that may have gone on for so long.

➢ Both parents and individuals may need special help to develop techniques for managing the patterns of behavior. In such cases, mental health professionals can counsel the child and the family, helping them to develop new skills, attitudes, and ways of relating to each other. In individual counseling, the therapist helps individuals with ADHD learn to feel better about themselves. The therapist can also help them to identify and build on their strengths, cope with daily problems, and control their attention and aggression.

Medications

- ➢ Medications help in the control and elimination of behavior, depression and other physical and psychiatric symptoms.
- ➢ Hope & Dreams fully, you will find a medicine, or group of medicine that will help you.
- ➢ It should not necessarily be a goal to stop medication—you may need to always take them, or change them as necessary, based on your physician.
- ➢ Remember, you have an **illness**, not a **weakness**—so needing medication is not bad.

The Medication Partnership

> Your goals: Feeling better
> Your psychiatric goal: Helping you feel better

Learn all you can about your prescribed medicines.

Take medications only through the prescriptions of a trusted doctor or psychiatrist.

Through education, find a medical physician who understands your condition and who can prescribe the proper medications for your condition needs.

Your psychiatrist expects you:

- ➢ To take the medicine exactly as prescribed
- ➢ To record any side effects
- ➢ To report immediately
  - o Any worsening symptoms
  - o Any intolerable side effects
- ➢ To consult with him or her in person or by phone about any changes in dosage or medicine.

Never analyze your symptoms and try to decide upon dosage or medicine by yourself.

Never take the medicine of another person.

If your physician or psychiatrist is not meeting your needs—remember, you're the boss!

Medications

Learning the following about each of your medications:
(A supporter may need to help you)

- ➤ Product name and its generic name
- ➤ Prescribed dosage level
- ➤ How does it work? What are the expectations?
- ➤ How soon will it work?
- ➤ What risks exist with the medicine?
- ➤ Does the medicine have a good track record?
- ➤ Why is it recommended?
- ➤ What are the side effects? Short term? Long term?
- ➤ Can the risk of the side effects be reduced?
- ➤ What dietary and lifestyle restrictions exist?
- ➤ How is the medication monitored?
- ➤ Is any pre-testing needed?
- ➤ What tests are needed while taking the medication? How often?
- ➤ What symptoms would indicate the need for a dosage change? A medicine change?
- ➤ How do I take the medication?

Look up your medicine in a medication reference book. Be sure to retain the insert of information that comes with the medicine package at the pharmacy.

Tips

➢ Develop a sure way of always taking your medicine correctly and on time.

➢ If blood testing is needed for your medication, be sure to have it done as specified. (Remember do not eat 24 hours prior to blood test).

➢ Work closely with a competent pharmacist.

➢ Be encouraged that medicines are always getting better.

➢ Discuss vitamins or supplements with your physician or med specialist, see if your pharmacist or your psychiatrist foresees possible medicine conflicts.

➢ Follow the lifestyle directives or your psychiatrist, such as:

▪ Diet limitations, rest, exercise, avoid caffeine, and avoid excess stress.

➢ No alcohol or illegal drugs.

Therapy

➢ Another key component that can help you attain your health wellness is individual therapy or counseling sessions with licensed therapist (a psychiatrist, counselor).

➢ Therapy helps us improve our mental well-being by analyzing our troublesome thoughts and feelings one-on-one with a professional and thinking and feeling better.

➢ Therapists can also help us with behavior and relationship difficulties.

➢ Sessions can be intense and therapy is hard work and there's always homework.

➢ Therapy can be of great benefits to us.

➢ Keep an open mind.

Therapy is an Achievement Tool!

Group Therapy

Is a session led by a trained mental health professional. There is complete confidentiality To include different, impartial viewpoints that can give you unbiased and beneficial feedback

Cognitive Therapy

The tactic of refuting negative thoughts, creating positive thoughts, and uncovering distorted thinking in a powerful therapeutic technique. It can be done one-on-one therapy sessions, or by yourself—it is an Achievement Tool. If you don't feel comfortable with the therapist, make a change.

Alternative Therapies

There are other health care professionals that don't practice medicine or conventional therapy. Alternative therapeutic treatments that they use include:

➢ Diet and nutrition

➢ Allergies (both food and other)

➢ Amino acids (organic)

➢ Vitamin and mineral supplements

➢ Hormones (chemical messengers in the body)

➢ Herbs (ask you doctor first)

➢ Controlling yeast infections

➢ Meditative exercises

➢ Bio-feedback

➢ Acupuncture

➢ Massage

Following an alternative therapeutic treatment plan works for many—it might for you. It could be one of your Achievement Tools.

Trauma

Abuse, victimization, neglect, or other traumatic experiences usually require **therapy** to improve thoughts, feelings, behaviors, and the **severe symptoms** they generate. Medicine can only help control the resultant symptoms.

Symptoms caused by trauma include:

Insomnia	Flashbacks
Anxiety	Passivity
Dissociation	Paranoia
Rage	Irritability
Numbing of emotions	Depression
Hyper-alertness	Bodily pain
Agitation/unrest	Intrusive memories
Isolation	Hyper-arousal
Substance abuse	

Kinds of Trauma

Child-abuse	Sexual abuse	Rape
Physical abuse	Rejection	Drug abuse
Aggressive acts	Natural disasters	Alcoholism
Co-dependency	Other compulsive behaviors	Child neglect
Spousal abuse	Marital difficulties	Verbal abuse
Personal loss or tragedy	Change in environment	War
Physical injury	Change in lifestyle	Terrorism
Death	Loss of Pet	Loss of Job

Recovering from Trauma

To recover from trauma, you must achieve:

Empowerment

You must be in charge of your healing, since control was taken from you by the experience.

Validation—Others must:

➤ Listen to you completely

➤ Validate the significance and importance of what has happened to you.

➤ Bear witness to your traumatic experience has had in you life.

➤ Understand the role that this traumatic experience has had in your life.

Connection—trauma left you bare and alone. You must reconnect with others.

1. Be supported

2. Be treated well

3. Be respected

Trauma Exercise

Few people recognize the impact of a traumatic event or deal with it directly, especially when the trauma is fresh. There are several reasons for this; one is that health care workers, family members and "uneducated" supporters tend to ignore the effects of trauma. They may tell the person who has been traumatized that the experience was their fault or to "forgive and forget and just get on with your life." This only makes the injured party feel invalidated and inappropriate for experiencing some very appropriate reactions.

Circle all below that you have experienced from the symptoms list?

- Mood instability

- Nightmares

- Flashbacks, intrusive thoughts, feeling, and Images

- Feeling on alert, hyper arousal

- Feeling unsafe in your body

- Feeling like your emotions, thought processes, and life are out of control

- Lack of self-confidence

- Unexplainable grief reactions

- Poor concentration

- Alcohol and substance abuse

- The impulse to engage in self-destructive acts

- Contemplating suicide or hurting someone else.

- Desire to hurt or mutilate yourself

- Lack of confidence in the future

- Uncontrolled fear

- Feeling that nothing makes sense

- Depression

- Insomnia

- Re victimization (abuse continues to occur)

- Feeling powerless to create change in your life

- Anxiety and panic attacks

- Dissociation from yourself and your life experiences

- Inability to experience pleasure

- Hopelessness

- Difficulty making decisions

- Food or other addictions

- A vague feeling that something unidentifiable is wrong

- Unexplainable outbursts of temper

- Inability to trust appropriate people

- Poor self-esteem

- Chronic muscle tension

Chapter 3
Achievement Tools

Achievement Tools

You have already heard of seven of our Achievement Tools:

Medicine	Support
Education	Alternative Therapy
Self-Advocacy	Diet and Nutrition
Therapy	

In General, wellness is most possible when you are doing:

➤ Things you enjoy.

➤ Things for yourself.

➤ Things that are useful .

➤ Things you need to be doing.

➤ Things by yourself.

➤ Things with or for others.

➤ Things you are responsible for doing.

➤ Anything that diverts focus from worrying about yourself.

Have a plan for each day to look forward to staying active-even busy.

Consider a night-time "winding down" activity
(Use the best suited for you and your needs)

Support	Things you like to do
Journaling	Relaxation and stress reduction exercises
Cognitive therapy	Light
Sleep	Sense of humor
Neatness, cleanliness and organization	Education
Artistic expression	Freeze Frame
Spirituality	Affirmations
Exercise	Diet and Nutrition
Avoiding vulnerability	Focusing

You may find other tools and techniques that can improve or maintain yourself-there are no rules—do what works for you.

Support Channels

Although we are in charge of our self maintenance, and growth, a critical component of our success is **support** from other. We need **support** from others such as:

Our Friends   Our Family

Our support Groups   Our peers

Our Health Care Professional   Our Support group

Even our pets

Support can lessen and even alleviate our psychiatric symptoms. For many of us support is the most effective and beneficial Achievement Tool.

Listening In Support Groups or Activities

In giving support to a friend on an individual basis, the most important skill you possess is **Listening!**

For someone to care about us and to listen completely and intently to us is a precious gift.

It allows us to fully express ourselves in any way- to talk about our problems and difficulties.

> ➤ Listening is a skill that must be developed.
>
> ➤ As listeners, it is not our responsibility to solve problems.
>
> ➤ Judgments, criticisms and unsolicited advice are inappropriate.
>
> ➤ We are **not** professionals- we are supporters.
>
> ➤ There should be complete confidentiality.

Support Channel Exercise

Circle all attributes you would want in your support team?

Mutual support   Someone who will listen

Counsel   Sharing

Diversion   Correspondence

Companionship   Understanding

Empathy   Advocacy activities

Play with you   Someone to talk to

Caring   Acceptance

Monitoring   Time affirm your individuality

Validate and encourage your dreams   Treat you with love, respect, and honesty

Accept your ups and downs without being judgmental

Who can help you as well as ask for your help

Be able to say "I understand what you are going through." And "I can see that this is really a difficult time for you."

Peer Counseling

(A **"peer"** is a friend who also has an illness who needs support)

Peer Supporters:

➤ First become friends.

➤ Agree to support each other

    o   Positively request support

    o   Positively offer support

➤ Agree on frequency of meetings and complete confidentiality.

➤ Agree that the time of the meeting will always be divided appropriately-how to split listening time.

➤ Meet in a comfortable, quiet place (private) or on the phone.

➤ Allow **no** distractions (TV, videos, phone calls, or music).

➤ Keep in touch when things are going well- that's a great time to do fun, exciting things together.

➤ Keep the relationship in balance- lunches, cards, surprises.

➤ Set appropriate boundaries (time to call...)

Peer counseling sessions can work with non-peer friends or supporters

Peer counseling is effective, safe, free and it works!

Peer Counseling Session

Listener listens:

- ➢ Providing positive support ONLY
- ➢ Providing comfort and safety
- ➢ Giving no judgment, criticism or advice
- ➢ Holding everything in strict confidence

Talker:

- ➢ Tries to use their time wisely
- ➢ Trusts the listener
- ➢ Talks about whatever they want to
- ➢ Can express an emotion:
  - o   Venting, crying, etc.
  - o   Emotion is never seen as a symptom
- ➢ Can be helped by the listener to find or focus upon the issue(s) that they met to talk about the most.

Begin session positively- What good things have happened?

End session positively- What are we looking forward to?

Be sensitive to difficulties in participation.

It is amazing what can be achieved just by having a friend listen to your issues, problems and feelings.

Supporters

Must take care of themselves:

➢ Have their own support

➢ Have realistic boundaries on their time

➢ Not allow themselves to be abused or overused

Should Not:

➢ Try to "rescue" a peer

➢ Do things for the peer that the peer could easily do for themselves

➢ Be an enabler for the peer

➢ Do things for the peer you don't want to do

➢ Make assumptions about what the peer needs- ask!

➢ Withhold information from the peer because of assumed effect

Should:

➢ Know everything about the peer (what to expect)

➢ Know the peer's doctors and the treatment strategies

Support Tips

1. Support is mutual and should be balanced.

2. We are they for each other in time of need.

3. Others are more likely to become friends and be supporters if we are positive and in charge of our illness—and have a plan or action.

4. We may have some inappropriate social skills that embarrass others and turn them off- we may have to take a risk and ask friends or health care professionals about this, and then with counseling, self-help books, awareness, and practice, bring about change.

5. Avoid wearing out a supporter- have 4 or 5!

6. Don't allow yourself to be abused by a supporter

7. Don't abuse or impose too much upon one person

8. It's wonderful to have a friend to call and to do something fun with.

Support Tips

When talking to a depressed person

Don't say:

You are the most depressed person I ever saw!

Oh, we all get depressed!

Why are you depressed?

You don't have anything to be depressed about!

But you are so competent- how can you put yourself in a position of such powerlessness?

You should take a vacation- get away from it all!

Just go take a hot bath and you'll feel better!

I don't believe in suicide- it a cowardly act!

What's the matter? Isn't your life exciting enough?

Pull yourself up by your bootstraps and get going!!

Say:

I'm sorry you are having such a hard time

What can I do to help?

I'm rooting for you!

Tell me how you feel- I'm here to listen!

You are special to me- please get well soon!

You will feel better-you will get well!

This must be a very hard time for you!

I love you and fully support you!

Support Groups

➤ Is a group of individuals or peers which meets on a regular basis.

➤ Is led by a peer facilitator.

➤ Offers no judgment, criticism, or advice- there are usually no professional present.

➤ Demands full confidentiality- with no exceptions.

➤ Allows attendance of non-individuals such as friends, family, health care workers, and supporters of any kind.

➤ Provides mutual support for all present and raises spirits.

Attendees:

➤ Attendance is optional..

➤ Everyone has an opportunity to speak in turn. Seating is often in a circle.

➤ Sharing is optional- it is neither encouraged nor discouraged.

➤ May talk about anything they want within reason.

➤ Is encouraged to offer supportive cross-talk:

   o Only one person speaks at a time

   o No side conversations are allowed

   o Do not make conversation about yourself

You can make new and lasting friendships at support groups!!!

Support from family

All individuals want from family members to:

Understand	Listen
Accept	Be available
Communicate	Show encouragement
Have compassion	Be attentive
Show love	Voice concerns
Patience	Validation

Some family members can provide some of these things, others cannot- they are human and could be in denial. Some of us have limited family or family living elsewhere.

We may enhance relationships with family members by:

➢ Promoting open discussions of the family

➢ Being supportive of them

➢ Planning activities, enjoying good times and appreciating each other.

➢ Meeting with the family and discussing:

o The support we need

o The support we can be given

o The support we can give

Making New Friends

Other ways of making new friends:

- ➤ Community activities
- ➤ Special interest groups
- ➤ Church groups
- ➤ Volunteer organizations

Be sure that your motivation for participating is both:

- ➤ Interest in the activity or group
- ➤ Interest in making new friends

Support from Health Care Professionals

We meet health care professionals who:

- ➢ Monitor us closely
- ➢ Emphasize self-care and self responsibility.
- ➢ Are willing to explore, try new approaches, and use less invasive alternatives
- ➢ Are willing to use a team approach
- ➢ Consider individual needs and preferences
- ➢ Have good listening and communication skills
- ➢ Care about us and accept us with compassion as we are
- ➢ Have positive hopes & dreams
- ➢ Encourage and understand us
- ➢ Admit and remedy mistakes
- ➢ Are friendly, supportive, and respectful
- ➢ Are firm and protective when necessary
- ➢ Are available and have back- up service
- ➢ Are up-to-date in their knowledge

Keep all appointments with health care professionals

If necessary, we may need to:

- ➢ Make an immediate appointment
- ➢ Schedule appointments more frequently

Support Groups Exercise

1. What do you get from support groups?

_____

_____

_____

_____

_____

_____

_____

2. What would you like to see in your group and why?

_____

_____

_____

_____

_____

_____

_____

3. How could you help make these changes happen?

_____

_____

_____

_____

_____

_____

_____

Family Support Exercise

1. Some people have said that their mood swings have had a great deal of negative impact on their family life, often creating complete havoc. The following is a list of these negative impacts and resulting emotions. Which ones apply to you and your family?

Disruption

Embarrassment

Overprotection

Tension, stress

Lack of trust

They are tired of me

Estrangement

Financially draining

Loss of hope

Fear

Unpleasantness

They feel helpless

They think it is all in my head

Everyone is affected by the stigma

Anxiety

Emotionally draining

Patronizing attitudes

Anger

Divorce

Was or became a dysfunctional family

Lack of understanding

Denial

Turmoil

Grief

Confusion

Exclusion

Worry

3. Some people said that family supporters actually strengthened their family relationships. Through developing more mutual understanding, becoming closer, and learning to communicate better. Which of the following apply to you and your relationship with your family?

Communication   Monitoring

Visiting   Tolerance

Counsel   Encouragement

Financial support   Understanding

Attention   Protection

Concern   Calling

Listening   Education

Living space   Availability

Writing   Love advice

Activities

Describe the other positive aspects of your relationship with your family and ways in which they have been supportive to you:

_____

_____

_____

_____

_____

_____

Describe any improvements in your relationship with your family and relative.

_____

_____

_____

_____

_____

_____

What do you feel is responsible for these improvements?

_____

_____

_____

_____

_____

_____

Is there anything you need to do to ensure that these improvements are maintained If so, what?

_____

_____

_____

_____

_____

_____

Education

As with support, **education** is both a growth concept and an important Achievement Tool.

The time we spend finding information, resources, learning about our illness, methods and tactics to use in controlling it is:

- ➢ Time well spent
- ➢ A positive, satisfying effort
- ➢ An achievement

It is empowering even to look up a word in the dictionary.

Things you like to do that divert your attention from yourself

Work at my job	Help someone in need
Listen to music	Build a model airplanes
Visit a friend	Gardening
Sew	Invite someone out for dinner
Write someone a letter	Go to a hobby store
Take a long walk	Visit a relative
Cook special meals & have people over	Watch your favorite TV show
Play basketball	Shop for groceries
Read	Go dancing
Plan and take a little trip alone or with someone	Play an instrument
Take a relaxing bath	Do arts and crafts
Off to my quiet place to be peaceful and think	Have a peer support session
Go to the mall to shop	Write in my journal

Creative Arts

The **creative arts** offer Achievement Tools that are very satisfying and powerful. They offer great potential for healing. We express our feelings, visions, hope & dreams, and fears in our artistic work.

Here are some examples of the creative arts:

Writing	Rapping	Writing songs
Woodworking	Landscaping	Pottery
Painting	Flower arranging	Dance
Jewelry making	Sculpting	Weaving
Drawing	Fabric art	Design pictures
Photo creativity on your computer		Playing musical instruments

There are many others as well!

Artistic Expression

If a creative art appeals to you, just start doing it playfully and expressively. Initially, don't worry about perfection or proper techniques- for healing to occur, just allow the natural process of creativity to happen.

➤ Don't judge yourself!

➤ Art is fun-try different materials and techniques

➤ **Everyone** has creativity within themselves

➤ Art is healing and therapeutic

➤ When you create art, you are uniquely expressing yourself.

➤ The uniqueness of your work can greatly enhance your self-esteem

Journaling/Writing

Many people enjoy, and are helped by journaling in a private book regularly every-day or whenever they want.

You can write:

➤ Whatever you want

➤ However you want

➤ As long as you want

Writing things down can help you:

➤ Put stressful things in perspective, lessening your anxiety and increasing calmness

➤ Become aware of things you don't realize

➤ See patterns of behavior in yourself and others

➤ See progress you are making as you look back at earlier entries

Any other type of writing is encouraged; cognitive therapy involves significant, focused writing. As with writing it is very creative and unique.

Journal Writing Exercise

1. Describe your experience of journaling.

_____

_____

_____

_____

_____

_____

_____

2. What role has journaling played in your wellness?

Relaxation and Stress Reduction Exercises

Relaxation and stress reduction exercises:

➤ Are useful tools in achieving recovery

➤ Can help you feel better about yourself

➤ Can help reduce or eliminate physical and physiological symptoms:

   o   Anxiety

   o   Agitation

   o   Stress

Learn how to relax by:

➤ Taking an educational course

➤ Renting an instructional video

➤ Listening to audio tapes and CD's

➤ Reviewing self-help books

Relaxation and Stress Reduction Techniques

Learn and practice relaxation techniques when you are feeling well. Practice them several times each day, in a quiet, comfortable place where you won't be interrupted. Then, when you actually need help relaxing or relieving stress, use the practiced techniques.

➤ Try a variety of relaxation tapes and see which ones work best for you.

➤ Progressive relaxation

➤ Body scan

➤ Guided imagery

➤ Checking in

➤ Freeze frame

Freeze—Frame

Recognize the stressful feeling and **Freeze-Frame** it. Make a sincere effort to shift your focus to the area around your heart. Pretend you are breathing through the heart to help you focus your energy in this area. Keep your focus there for 10 seconds or more.

Recall a fun, positive feeling or time you had in your life and attempt to re-experience it.

Now, using your intuition, common sense and sincerity, ask your self what would be a more efficient response to the situation- one that would minimize future stress? Listen to what your self says in answer to your questions.

From the book: *Freeze-Frame: One Minute Stress Management*

Focusing

Focusing is a simple, safe, free, & non-invasive, yet powerful self-help technique that can help reduce physical and psychological symptoms. The focusing sequence uses a series of well-defined questions or steps to help us focus on the "real" issues. One of the most importance at any given time not what we may be thinking 'should" be the real issue. It connects us with the feelings generated by the issue. When connecting with the feelings are made and explored, a positive change in feeling is often achieved. The result is an understanding at a new level that translates into feeling better and, a reduction of our psychological symptoms.

Get ready for a focusing exercise by setting down in a comfortable space and asking yourself: "how does it feel inside my body right now?" Search around inside your body to notice any feelings of uneasiness or discomfort and focus your attention on these feelings for a few moments.

Ask yourself: "What's between me and feeling fine?" Do not answer- let the feeling that comes in your body do the answering? As each concern comes up, put it aside, like making a mental list. Ask yourself, "Except for these things, am I fine?" Review the list. See which problem stands out and seems to be begging for your attention. It may be different from the one you thought was most important. Ask yourself if it is okay to focus on the problem. If the answer is "yes", notice what you sense in your body when you recall the whole of that problem. (If the answer is "no", choose another problem that stands out and let the first problem alone for the time being.) Sense all the feelings of the problem. Really feel it in your body for several minutes.

Let a word, phrase or image that matches the feeling of this problem come into your mind. Go back and forth between the word, phrase or image. Do they really match? If they don't find another word, phrase, or image that does feel like a match. When they match, go back and forth several times between the word or phrase or image and the feeling in your body. If the feeling in your body changes, follow it with your attention-notice it. Be with the feeling for several moments.

If you want, ask yourself the following questions about the problem to help yourself get a change in the way you feel:

> ➢ How does my body feel?

> ➢ What needs to happen inside me for this feeling to change?

> ➢ What would feel like a small step forward?

> ➢ What would feel like a fresh perspective?

> ➢ How would I feel inside if this were all okay?

> ➢ What needs to change inside me for me to feel better?

Be with the feelings that come up for a few moments. Then ask yourself, "Am I ready to stop or should I do another round of focusing?" If you are going to stop, relax for a few minutes and notice how your feelings have changed-before resuming your regular activities.

Spirituality

> ➢ We each may find tremendous strength in the spirituality Achievement Tool.

> ➢ Each of us needs to explore and find our own true feelings about religion and meaning of life. (If we wish, we might not have a spirituality tool.)

> ➢ However, our spiritual feelings may give us a strong sense of purpose, self- worth, value and significance.

> ➢ These feelings can boost our self-esteem!

> ➢ Explore your spirituality.

> ➢ Find what you believe and enjoy every moment of your life!

> ➢ Religion & spirituality are not the same.

Affirmations

Affirmations are positive statements about ourselves that we fully believe. They could begin with our own thoughts or thoughts shared with us by others. They should be written down so that we can refer to them when we want or need to.

An affirmation is:

- ➤ Created
- ➤ Scrutinized, examined and validated with time
- ➤ Internalized and fully believed

Going over affirmations is a wonderful Achievement Tool because it reinforces our value and self-esteem.

Referring to our affirmations is a good daily activity-even multiple times-and could be part of a night-time activity

Cognitive Therapy

Our thoughts lead to our feelings. Negative thoughts lead to negative feelings. Cognitive therapy involves changing negative thoughts to positive.

- ➤ Is complementary to medication and other counseling
- ➤ Requires concentrated thinking and a level of wellness
- ➤ Is intense- so beware of burnout
- ➤ Should be tailored to our needs
- ➤ Can be done through individual therapy sessions-or alone with silence and complete concentration.

Is presented in numerous self-help books such as:

Thoughts and Feelings by Mathew McKay, Ph.D., Martha Davis, Ph. D., and Patrick Fanning

The Feeling Good Handbook by David Burns, M.D.

Feeling Good by David Burns, M.D.

These are workbooks with reinforcement exercises- they are adaptable to a model using weekly lessons with homework.

Cognitive Therapy Writing

Cognitive therapy requires the writing down of the negative thoughts you are trying to get rid of and your positive rebuttals to those thoughts.

Note paper, a notebook, a journal, or a computer should be used. Keep all writing.

➢ Track progress in your thinking.

➢ Potentially help you again with the same or similar thoughts.

A tape recorder might be of use for repetition.

Negative Thoughts

Are specific discrete messages	Are believed, no matter how irrational
May include should, ought, must	Are idiosyncratic
Are learned	Are shorthand
Are automatic	Are spontaneous
Are hard to turn off	Can be unlearned

Examples of Negative Thoughts

"I will never be stable"	"I am stupid"
"I am a complete failure"	"No one would ever love (or like) me"
"I will never be good enough"	"I will never meet life goals"
"I can't do anything right"	"I mess up everything"
"I don't deserve to be alive"	

"I will never accomplish anything worthwhile"

Find and uncover your negative thoughts-

➤ In therapy

➤ With peers, friends and family

➤ By yourself

Negative thought patterns

➤ **Filtering:** looking at one part of a situation to the exclusion of everything else.

➤ **Polarized thinking:** perceiving things as the extreme, as either black or white, with no in-between.

➤ **Over generalizing:** reaching a broad, generalized conclusion based on just one piece of evidence

➤ **Mind Reading:** Making assumptions about how others feel based on insufficient evidence.

➤ **Catastrophizing:** expecting the worst to happen

➤ **Personalizing:** relating everything to oneself, including continual comparison of oneself to others.

➤ **Controlling:** feeling either totally controlled by an outside force that you are responsible for everything.

➤ **Fallacy of fairness:** thinking that everything must be fair or equal

➤ **Emotional reasoning:** believing that everything felt must be true

➤ **Fallacy of change:** assuming happiness depends on the actions of others and that if they would change, things would improve.

➤ **Blaming:** making someone else responsible

➤ **Shoulds:** operating from a rigid set of indisputable rules about how everyone should act.

➤ **Being right:** continually needing to prove that one's view or action are right, even though evidence indicates the contrary.

➤ **Perfectionism:** expecting never to make mistakes, always to be perfect

Negative Thoughts Exercise

1. Filtering entails looking at only one part of a situation to the exclusion of everything else.

   _____

   _____

   _____

   _____

   _____

   _____

2. Think of an example when you filtered your thoughts:

   _____

   _____

   _____

   _____

   _____

   _____

3. Identify the distorted perception in your example:

   _____

   _____

   _____

   _____

   _____

   _____

4. How did you feel when you filtered your thoughts in this way?

_____

_____

_____

_____

_____

_____

5. When you filter your thoughts does it ever cause conflict between yourself and others?

_____

_____

_____

_____

_____

_____

6. Describe examples of this:

_____

_____

_____

_____

_____

_____

Analysis and Rebuttal

Analyze your negative thoughts- one at a time.

➢ Does it fit a negative thought pattern?

➢ Would a kind person think this of another?

➢ Does it contain inflammatory words? (Loser, jerk, stupid, terrible, etc.)

➢ Who gave me this thought? What is going on?

➢ What pain am I experiencing from it?

Examining the thought in a different light can help.

➢ Develop a set of positive rebuttals to your negative thought.

➢ Avoid negative terms such as: not, never, can't, upset, etc.

➢ Be sure the statement is positive and in the present tense.

o Example: "I am doing an excellent job."

Examples of positive rebuttals

Negative thought: "I will never be well or stable"
Positive Rebuttal: "I am well", "I am stable"

Negative thought: "I am not worth anything"
Positive Rebuttal: "I am a valuable person"

Negative thought: "I have never accomplished anything"
Positive Rebuttal: "I have accomplished many things"

Negative thought: "It is not OK to make a mistake"
Positive Rebuttal: "It is OK to make mistakes"

Negative thought: "I want to die"
Positive Rebuttal: "I choose life"

Reinforce Rebuttals

Reinforce your positive rebuttals:

- ➢ Repeating them aloud
- ➢ Thinking of them repeatedly
- ➢ Writing them down repeatedly
- ➢ Playing them again and again on a tape recorder
- ➢ Posting them in key places, observing them often

The negative thought:

- ➢ Has been deep-rooted
- ➢ Has been "learned" and fully accepted
- ➢ Will fade and die as your positive thoughts become part of what you believe

Your positive thoughts become affirmations- things about yourself that you believe!!

Light

Some of us get more and more depressed, anxious and lethargic as the days get shorter and darker-when the weather is dark and dreary for extended periods of time. This is known as **SAD**- the seasonal affective disorder.

➤ Have your doctor diagnose this illness and refer you to an expert in this field.

➤ Use a "vita light" or full-spectrum light, as necessary.

➤ Distorted spectrum light- like older fluorescent light, can make us jittery and uneasy (not just when it's broken and blinking), so try to avoid it.

➤ Get outside into the light as much as possible.

➤ Let light get into your eyes-remove glasses/sunglasses.

➤ Never look directly into the sun.

➤ Sit or work near windows- you need to always have as much light as possible.

➤ Others get depressed at only certain times of the year.

Light Exercise

Read through the statements below, and then spend as much time as you need to determine whether or not they're true of you. You might want to consult old journals and calendars in thinking about your answers.

_____I notice that I have more problems with depression in the late fall and early winter.

_____I notice that my mood is lower on cloudy days and worsen when there is a series of cloudy days.

_____I notice that I feel better on bright sunny days and when I get some light during the day.

_____I plan to be outside for at least half an hour every day (I can get both the exercise and light needed during a half-hour walk)

_____After two weeks of increased exposure to full-spectrum light, I've noticed the following changes:

_____After two months of increased exposure to full-spectrum light, I've notice the following changes:

_____I intend to make the following changes in my daily routine based on my observations of how I felt after two months of increased exposure to full-spectrum light:

Exercising

Exercise is a great anti-depressant an example of—**physical** activity improving your **mental** state of mind.

➢ Helps maintain and strengthen your body

➢ Strengthen muscles and organs

➢ Helps you lose weight

➢ Helps you control your blood cholesterol levels

➢ Helps increase endurance and coordination

➢ Can lengthen your life- you only have one body

➢ Can be done with others, providing fun and social interaction

➢ 20 minutes of aerobic workout is great (heart, lungs, and oxygen intake)

➢ You have become an exerciser when you begin to ask the question **"When?" and not the questions "Whether?"**

Exercise-Getting Started

It's hard to get started-begin gradually without overdoing it. Get your doctor's approval before starting any exercise program.

Choose the exercises that are best for you:

➢ Walking, running or jogging

➢ Biking, swimming or gym workouts

Other exercise disciplines, psychological exercise:

➢ Can help you avoid and lower stress

➢ Can reduce and prevent psychological symptoms

➢ Can stimulate endorphins

o Having a pain-relieving affect

o With peptide 9 amino acids, proteins

➢ Can raise your self-esteem

➢ Allows quality time with your very best friend—(you can have a private peer counseling session).

Exercising Exercise

There is a universal agreement that exercise makes people feel better. If they are depressed, exercise improves their mood. If they are manic, gentle exercise, such as a leisurely walk, helps calm them down.

Varying the kind of exercise you do from day to day may make the regimen more interesting for you. On the other hand, when you are depressed, the same thing over and over, every day, can feel easier and more comfortable. Whatever works best for you is what you need to do.

1. If you have a hard time exercising when you are depressed, do you think this is a problem for you?

    _____

    _____

    _____

    _____

    _____

    _____

2. What could you do for yourself that would make it easier to exercise when you are depressed?

    _____

    _____

    _____

    _____

    _____

    _____

It helps to have a regularly scheduled time to exercise. Walking for half an hour at lunchtime works for some people. Others prefer to exercise early in the morning or in the late afternoon. If you exercise consistently at a particular time, the regimen becomes a habit. Even if you miss a day or two a week, you'll still reap enormous benefits. Remember: It is always a good idea to get your doctor's approval before increasing your activity level, especially if you have a medical condition requiring treatment.

3. How would you rate your current fitness level? Check the one that applies.

_____I feel that I am already getting all the exercise I need.

_____I feel that I need to increase the amount of exercise I get.

You can determine if you are really out of shape and need more exercise by considering the following symptoms. Check the ones that apply to you.

_____Out of breath after walking up a flight of stairs or climbing a hill.

_____Feeling exhausted after short periods of exertion.

_____Chronic muscle tension

_____Poor muscle tone

_____Obesity

_____Muscles are cramped and ache for days after participating in a sport

_____Generally tired, lethargic and bored

_____Other symptoms you have which might be due to lack of exercise:

Enjoy yourself while exercising. Consider this as special time that you are giving to yourself and your body. If you have not been exercising regularly, start slowly and increase your time and exertion gradually. At first you may be able to exercise for only five minutes. Age and physical shape make a difference. Try exercising for five minutes three times a day. Then, try increasing your time to ten minutes each time.

1. How I felt before I began a program of regular exercise:

_____

_____

_____

_____

_____

_____

2. How I felt after exercising regularly for two weeks:

_____

_____

_____

_____

_____

_____

3. After exercising when depressed I felt:

_____

_____

_____

_____

_____

4. After exercising when manic I felt:

_____

_____

_____

_____

_____

My long-term exercise goals are:

_____

_____

_____

Sleep

Sleep is a unique Achievement Tool in that we are not conscious when we are doing it. We and everyone else, can only have Hope & Dreams that we sleep regularly! It is basic, underlying importance that we sleep in order to function well the next day. Physicians usually will try to stabilize a patient's sleep early in their treatment

What difficulties have you had with sleep?

➢ Sleeping more than usual.

➢ Having a difficult time getting to sleep.

➢ Having a difficult time getting up in the morning.

➢ Awakening often in the night.

➢ Having bad dreams during sleep awaking very early and being unable to go back to sleep.

Tactics for Better Sleep

➢ Going to bed at the same time every night.

➢ Getting up at the same time every morning.

➢ Trying to avoid odd hours and shift work

➢ Avoiding alcohol and drugs.

➢ Taking supplement medications (vitamins, minerals, herbs, hormones) only with your doctor's approval!

➢ Eating regularly and well.

➢ Eating your evening meal early-make it light "not heavy".

➢ Having adequate calcium intake.

➢ Avoiding weight-loss programs that might cause you to awaken early because you are hungry.

➢ Avoiding strenuous exercise before bed-time.

➢ Avoid caffeine before bed time.

- ➢ Creating a good sleeping environment:
  - o Proper bed
  - o No noise
  - o No light
  - o Proper temperature

The night-time activity objective:

- ➢ To wind down
- ➢ To relieve the pace, stress and anxiety of the day
- ➢ To lessen or remove any negative feelings

Possible Tactics:

- ➢ Reading or Journaling
- ➢ Listening to a relaxation tape
- ➢ Listening to soothing, calming music
- ➢ Watching TV shows you enjoy
- ➢ Cognitive therapy for a troubling negative thought
- ➢ Studying and focusing upon your affirmations
- ➢ Creating a new affirmation
- ➢ Talking to someone you love
- ➢ Planning your first activity for the morning
- ➢ Eating a turkey sandwich with a glass of milk
- ➢ Taking a warm, relaxing bath with lavender oil
- ➢ Rubbing your chest with lavender oil
- ➢ Drinking a cup of chamomile tea
- ➢ Using melatonin, with doctor's agreement

Diet and Nutrition

This lesson will provide information on how to eat properly. There will be no information on dieting, per se. Rather, eating properly should be taught in the context of being health and how that improved health is important for job performance. Information from the lesson title "Fitness" and providing information on reducing calories in this lesson should give people enough information of losing weight. The information on the Food Pyramid Guide is from the Center for Nutrition Policy and Promotion, which is an agency within the United States Department of Agriculture.

1. Meet with the members of the class for a short introductory session. During this meeting, the trainer should introduce the lesson and instruct the students that they should keep tRack of the food and beverages they consumer each day for a week. Give them the recording form that is provided. For students who have difficulty writing, instruct them to have someone help them record what they eat. If this assignment is too difficult for most of the class members, skip this step and adjust the lesson accordingly.

2. Using the information contained in the materials on the Food Guide Pyramid, provide instruction on how to maintain a balanced diet. Use visual aids as needed. Discuss each of the six different food groups, what foods are in each group, and about how much they should have from each group each day. Providing information on the exact amount of servings that are recommended may get too complex for many students, so try to provide general guidelines. For example, "it is important that you eat more servings from the bread group than the meat group. Try to eat a few fruits and vegetables each day and very little fat or sugar."

3. Discuss calorie intake. Calories are the fuel that the body needs to burn up provide energy. Energy allows us to be more productive, alert, and think better. If people are getting their "energy" fro sugar, nicotine, and caffeine, hey should be informed that this provides short-term "energy" which requires continuous consumption of these products to keep that false sense of energy. In order to have "good energy," a person needs to consume health calories. This is accomplished by eating 2,000-3,000 healthy calories throughout the day. People should eat breakfast, lunch, and dinner with a few healthy snacks in between.

Counting calories can be complex and tedious, so use the information provided to teach some basic guidelines. People get their calories from three basic sources: carbohydrates, protein, and fats. There is much debate about what percentage of a person's daily intake should come from each source of calories. Most guidelines suggest that 50-60 percent of your calories should come from carbohydrates (breads, grain, fruits, and vegetables) and the other 40-50 percent should come from protein (cheese, meat, milk) and fat (butter, lard, oil). Instruct students that a person gets more energy when they burn calories from carbohydrates and protein. Yet, fat contains twice as many calories per gram as the other two. By eating a greater percentage of carbohydrates and protein, the person gets more energy from fewer calories.

Remind students that they still need to be concerned with calories. If you consume 3,000 healthy calories a day and only burn 2,500 calories, you are still going to gain weight. Nevertheless, due the following examples due to stress that eating properly allows a person to consume more food and still be healthy. If a person starts the day with a sausage biscuit with egg at a local fast food place, he has just consumed more than a fourth of the recommended calories (56) and over half the recommended fat (35 grams). This means that he has used up quite a bit of his daily allowance on a little, probably unsatisfying breakfast. A bowl of breakfast food, banana, and glass of juice would provide the person more energy from fewer calories and almost no fat. It is important to stress balance. Having a Big Mac every once in a while is not going to be a big deal. The idea is to get students to adopt a lifestyle that includes a well-balanced diet most of the time.

4.   Discuss that a well-balanced diet also is important for other health concerns. When it comes to nutrition, people generally think only about body weight. However, a person who is thin and eating a lot of fatty foods is putting himself at risk of having health problems such as high blood pressure and high cholesterol, which can lead to heart attacks. Some people have medical conditions, such as diabetes, that require them to follow a strict diet. It is important to stress the importance of following a doctor's recommended diet. When a person does not do that, he puts himself at risk for serious health problems. Remind people that it is hard to be successful at work when they are using many sick days due to illness that can be prevented by a proper diet.

5. In order to review some of the concepts discussed, review the nutritional contents of different food products. This will also provide training on how to read food labels. Some important figures to look at include the serving size, number of calories from fat compared to the total calories, and percentage of the daily allowance from fat, cholesterol sodium, carbohydrates and protein. A healthy food should have a small percentage of its calories from fat, little to no saturated fat, cholesterol and sodium. Try to find foods that contribute more than 25 percent of the daily recommended allowance of fat, cholesterol, or sodium in one serving. These foods will help illustrate that sometimes eating a small amount of tasty food can put a huge dent into the total amount of nutrients a person should eat each day. Point out serving sizes. The amount of calories in a bag of chips might be reasonable based on its serving size. However, if the serving size is three chips, it only takes a few handfuls before the amount of calories is unreasonable.

6. For those students who completed a daily food intake form, have them review their information and discuss. Are they eating a healthy diet? What can they do to improve the balance of their diet? Have them look at one meal that was particularly unhealthy and see if they come up with an alternative, more healthy meal.

Many people understand what makes up a healthy diet, but they choose to indulge in foods that tend to be unhealthy. The students will have the knowledge to adopt a healthy diet if they choose. If a student does choose to eat more sensibly, they seek out assistance or do it on their own.

Diet and Nutrition (continues)

Food categories are:

Proteins: Dairy, meat, fowl, fish, eggs, grains, nuts, amino acids, beans (4 calories per gram).

Carbohydrates: sugars, starches, fruits, vegetables,—energy!

Fats: Butter, margarine, vegetable oils; (9 calories per gram)

Fibers: found in fruit and vegetables

Vitamins: organic substances grown in nature

Minerals: In-organic substances (not grown in nature)

WATER is important in nearly every bodily process. Drink at least 6 (8 oz) glasses per day.

Consume only as many calories as you need. What we eat definitely affects how we feel!!

Avoid:
- ➢ Eating any one food excessively or exclusively
- ➢ Over-eating or under-eating
- ➢ Having too great sugar intake
- ➢ Having too great salt intake
- ➢ **Caffeine:** it can cause or worsen psychiatric symptoms, such as anxiety or panic
- ➢ **Nicotine:** a strong stimulant that can cause or increase anxiety
- ➢ Stimulant medications, such as appetite suppressants (any medications containing amphetamines) except those prescribed by your doctor.

Avoid these:

> MSG—monosodium glutamate (preservative)
> BHA—antioxidant—a preservative
> BHT antioxidant—an additive

- ➢ Artificial colors and flavoring
- ➢ Hormones in meat
- ➢ Not chewing food well
- ➢ Drinking too much liquid with a meal
- ➢ Eating too fast or on the run

Diet Facts

- Double Whopper with Cheese
  - Calories: 960
  - Fat Grams: 63
- Medium fries
  - Calories:230
  - Fat Grams: 13
- Medium chocolate shake
  - Calories:320
  - Fat Grams: 7
- Dutch apple pie
  - Calories:300
  - Fat Grams: 15
- Celery stalk
  - Calories:5
  - Fat Grams: 0
- Cooked cauliflower
  - Calories:30
  - Fat Grams: 0
- Carrot
  - Calories:30
  - Fat Grams: 0
- Snap-beans (cups)
  - Calories:45
  - Fat Grams: 0
- Brewed coffee 9cup)
  - Calories: 5
  - Fat Grams: 0
- Half-and-half (1T)
  - Calories: 20
  - Fat Grams: 2
- Haagen-Dazs ice cream bar
  - Calories: 390
  - Fat Grams: 27

Diet and Nutrition Exercise

Instructions: Each day, write down what you eat at breakfast, lunch and dinner. Also write down what you eat in between meals. See example.

Day _Monday_
Breakfast _2-eggs, 2 pieces of bacon, 1—piece of toast and a glass of milk. (1 or 2%/whole)_
Lunch _Big Mac, large fries, large coke_
Dinner _2 plates of spaghetti, 5 pieces of bread, and 2 glasses of Kool Aid_
In Between Meals _Candy bar, apple pie and cookies_

Day _____
Breakfast _____
Lunch _____
Dinner _____
In Between Meals _____

Day _____
Breakfast _____
Lunch _____
Dinner _____
In Between Meals _____

Day _____
Breakfast _____
Lunch _____
Dinner _____
In Between Meals _____

Day _____
Breakfast _____
Lunch _____
Dinner _____
In Between Meals _____

Day _____
Breakfast _____
Lunch _____
Dinner _____
In Between Meals _____

Day _____
Breakfast _____
Lunch _____
Dinner _____
In Between Meals _____

Day _____
Breakfast _____
Lunch _____
Dinner _____
In Between Meals _____

Day _____
Breakfast _____
Lunch _____
Dinner _____
In Between Meals _____

Other Diet Tips

➢ Increase your intake of raw and fresh vegetables

➢ Reduce your intake of foods that contain animal fat cholesterol

➢ Focus on a daily diet that include:
  o Five servings of vegetables
  o Six servings of complex carbohydrates (whole grains)
  o Smaller amounts of protein

➢ Explore (keeping your doctor informed) supplementary items:
  o Vitamins (particularly "B complex")
  o Minerals
  o Amino acids
  o Herbs
  o Enzymes

Diabetic Constraints

If you have **hypoglycemia** (periodic drops in blood sugar level).

You should avoid:

➢ All simple sugars
➢ Dried fruits

And you should:

➢ Dilute fruit juices with water
➢ Substitute whole grain foods for refined carbohydrates.
➢ Have a healthy snack between meals or eat 4 or 5 smaller meals each day.

If you have **hyperglycemia** (diabetes—blood sugar levels too high)
(Take medications as prescribed and wear alert bracelet)

➢ Eliminate sugar and refined flour (white)
➢ Take insulin by pill or injection

If you suspect you might be allergic to some foods, try to isolate the food allergy by:

➢ Eliminating and Observation
➢ Reintroduction and Observation

Sense of Humor

Laughter

- ➤ Is a good medicine
- ➤ Can make life much more fun
- ➤ Is a powerful Achievement Tool

Depression and psychiatric symptoms can silently take our sense of humor from us It maybe impossible for us:

- ➤ To laugh
- ➤ Even to smile

Fight for your sense of humor!

Making someone else laugh is good for you. Find a friend that helps you laugh at little things and at life.

Sense of Humor Exercise

Researchers have found that a hearty laugh is one of the least expensive treatments for pent-up anxiety, fear and frustration. Laughing improves respiration because as you laugh, your lungs keep filling with fresh air and expelling the stale air. Laughter also increases your heart rate temporarily, in proportion to the duration of you laughter. This is actually good for you, because after you stop laughing, your heart rate drops below what it was before something struck you as funny. If that is not enough, a hearty belly laugh almost always results in total body relaxation.

1. What makes you laugh?

_____

_____

_____

_____

_____

2. When you laugh, how did you feel before you started laughing?

_____

_____

_____

_____

_____

_____

3. How did you feel after you laughed?

_____

_____

_____

_____

_____

_____

Neatness

Our personhood

o   Being clean, well-groomed and well-dressed can help make us feel good about ourselves.

Our personal surroundings

o   Living in and working in a clean, neat and organized environment can help keep our mood high.

Avoid Vulnerabilities

Alcohol abuse	Drug abuse
Diet abuse	Medicine non-compliance
Financial irresponsibility	Doing dangerous things
Excessive caffeine	Toxic relationships

Taking risk that could end badly

Making poor decisions-**not** doing what is in your best interest

Neatness—continued

Each Mind Is a Treed Lawn

➢   Leaves fall on every lawn (problems, pain, etc.)

➢   There are proven techniques for gathering leaves

➢   Wind can be a problem

➢   Our minds have lost of wind
o   Calm your wind
o   Control your mind
o   **Practice LIFE CHANGING SELF AWARENESS**

➢   You cannot rake blowing leaves

Chapter 4
Your Life Changing Self Awareness Daily Self-Plan

Your Life Changing Self Awareness Daily Self-Plan

- ➢ Customization of your life
- ➢ Our Achievement Tools
- ➢ The Improvement File
- ➢ Daily Growth Plan
- ➢ Risk
- ➢ Trigger Points
- ➢ When things are not going good in my life
- ➢ Control

Plan Supplies

All you need to develop your own recovery monitoring system are:

- ➢ A 3-ring binder-1" works best
- ➢ A set of 6 tabbed dividers
- ➢ A package of three holed filler paper
- ➢ A writing instrument of some kind
- ➢ Optional—a friend or other supporter to give you assistance and feedback

Development Plan

- ➢ When things are not going good in my life
- ➢ Supporters/Support Channel
- ➢ Respite Care
- ➢ Help From Others
- ➢ Help From Others
- ➢ Warning Signs
- ➢ Medication
- ➢ Treatment Facilities

Customization of your Life Development Plan

Each of our life "signatures" is different:

➢ We have different life's

➢ We have unique symptoms

➢ Respond to different things

➢ Respond differently to things

➢ Benefit from different Achievement Tools

➢ Benefit differently from an Achievement Tool

Through experimentation—trying different Achievement Tools——we will find the Achievement Tools that work best for you.

In the **LIFE CHANGING SELF AWARENESS** development plans, we specify events or symptoms we are vulnerable to (different for each of us) and actions we plan to take in each such circumstance (from the Achievement Tools).

Thus, each plan is customized and unique.

This is an on-going work in progress for the rest of your life.

Our Achievement Tools

On TAB 1 "Write" Our Achievement Tools. These are all of the tools that can help us during our recovery for independence and a better quality of life.

The Improvement File

On TAB 2 "Write" Our Achievement Tools.

Why not keep everything together in one place?

- Our six plans
- Our Achievement Tools and tailored usage information
- Our numbers to call in case of an emergency
- Support Channel Individuals
- Friends, peers, churches, family and health care professionals
- Doctor's information
- Educational information you have gained—and test results
- Medical test results you have received
- Medicine instructions and information
- Therapy objectives and goals
- Our affirmations
- Our pictures of loved ones

Daily Growth Plan
"Independence is around the corner"

On the first page, describe yourself when things are going well in your life. (Do it in a list form)

Some descriptive words that others have used are:

Bright	Cheerful	Talkative	Outgoing
Boisterous	Energetic	Humorous	Happy
Dramatic	Athletic	Optimistic	Reasonable
Responsible	Complete	Industrious	Compulsive
Content	Calm	Quiet	Introverted
Withdrawn	Reserved	Curious	Active

Daily Growth Plans

➤ The things you do when '*things are going well in your life*"

➤ Label the first tab—Daily Growth Plan

➤ How do you "carry out" a good day?

➤ Different "type" days can have different Daily Growth Plans

Daily Growth Plan "Must Do's"

On the next page make a list of things you need to do for yourself everyday to keep your life going down the correct path for success in life.

**1) Get out of bed   2) Make my Bed   3) Personal Hygiene practices
4) Get dressed   5) Go outside for work or school**

➤ Eat three healthy meals and two healthy snacks
➤ Drink at least six (8 oz) glasses of water
➤ Exercise for at least 30 minutes
➤ Get half-an-hour exposure to outdoor light
➤ Take medications, vitamins, and minerals
➤ Get 20 minutes of relaxation or meditation daily
➤ Write in journal for at least 15 minutes
➤ Spend 30 minutes enjoying a fun, affirming, or creative activity

Daily Growth Plan "Might Do's"

- ➢ Set up an appointment with a health care professional
- ➢ Spend time with a good friend
- ➢ Spend extra time with my partner, relatives and friends
- ➢ Get in touch with my family
- ➢ Spend individual time with pets
- ➢ Do peer counseling with a supporter or friend
- ➢ Get more sleep
- ➢ Go grocery shopping
- ➢ Have some personal time for yourself
- ➢ Make fun plans for the weekend
- ➢ Make plans when you get out of school or from work
- ➢ Plan a vacation or trip
- ➢ Take a hot bubble bath
- ➢ Go to a support group or twelve step meeting

Daily Growth Plan "Growth/Risk Do's"

Ask for:

Help	Advice	Introduce yourself	Permission
Job	Date		

Do something:

- ➢ Extra that you weren't asked to do
- ➢ That needs doing
- ➢ For the first time

Risk

➤ If you succeed—wonderful!

➤ If you are not successful—

   o   You tried, try again

   o   It'll be easier next time!

   o   You learned a lot from the positive and negative aspect of the situation

➤ Do "Growth/Risks" completely at your own pace

➤ Maintenance is fine

➤ But we can and will grow!

Triggers

External events or circumstances which produce serious outcome that make you feel like you are having a bad day. These may be normal reactions to events in our lives, but if we don't respond to them and deal with them in some way, they may actually worsen the problem.

On the third tab, write "Triggers" and put in several sheets of notebook paper

Examples:

➤ Loss or trauma or anniversary of loss or trauma

➤ Long, hard, tiring, repetitious work or too much stress

➤ Family friction

➤ Isolating

➤ Upsetting meeting or appointment

➤ Being teased, put down, or judged

➤ Being irritated by someone or others

➤ Physical illness or impairment

➤ Loud noises or disruption of calm

➤ Abandonment—or reminders of abandonment

➢ Traumatic news

➢ Relationship ending

➢ Financial problems or over-spending

➢ Sexual harassment

➢ Substance abuse such as alcohol or drugs

➢ Increasing in smoking

➢ Over-eating or under-eating

➢ Not answering the phone

➢ Acting dangerously or taking chances

Trigger Points

➢ Trigger Points are internal and may be unrelated to reactions to stressful situations.

➢ In spite of our best efforts at reducing symptoms, we may begin to experience Trigger Points—subtle signs of change that indicate we may need to take some further action.

➢ Fill in second tab.

Examples:

Anxiety or irritability

Aches and pains

Feeling left out

Feeling over stressed

Being uncaring, unmotivated, apathetic

Nervousness

Weepiness

Feeling guilt

Feeling angry

Feeling unconnected to body

Lack of concentration

Negative thoughts

Feeling inadequate

Feeling overwhelmed

Inability to experience pleasure

Feeling discouragement or Hope & Dreams

Irrational thoughts

Feeling worthlessness

Feeling shame

Feeling slowed-down or sped-up

Being obsessed with something unimportant

Triggers "Must Do's"

<u>Triggers</u>	<u>Actions to Take</u>
Isolation	Force socialization or help someone or call a friend and visit.
Family friction	Visit with apology and food and/or flowers
Sexual harassment	Assert myself and get what I need/deserve
Acting dangerously	Take care of myself and do what is in my best interest safety-wise.
Being teased, judged	Go over affirmations
Loss/anniversary of loss	Allow grief, and thoughts, and take care of yourself
Any trigger	Carry out a Daily Growth Plan
Negative thoughts	Rest and read my affirmations, the positive thoughts about myself that I know and believe.
Irritability	Change environment, be alone and calm down
Being uncaring	Help or be nice to someone
Being nervous	Use the "Pounding Surf" audio tape, twice
Feeling worthlessness	Help my neighbor
Any early warning sign	Carry out a daily Growth Plan

Can you change your plan? YES! But you can't give up!

Triggers "Might Do's"

Triggers	Actions to Take
Relationship ending	Move back home or begin a new relationship without moving.
Family friction	Move away or reset priorities
Substance abuse	Change environment or change relationships or get help immediately.
Disruption of calm	Change environment immediately or take prescribed medications.
Long hard work	Take a "health" break or take a trip for fun or quit and work somewhere else.
Being judged or teased	Make some new affirmations
Feeling worthless	Visit relatives or friends, clean out the garage, work on landscaping your yard or work on affirmations.
Negative thoughts	Concentrate on disregarding negative thoughts and finding new affirmations.
Weepiness	Force yourself to read or write in your journal or do some physical exercise, take a nap.

When things in your life are breaking down

In spite of our best efforts, our life problems may progress to the point where they are very uncomfortable, serious, and even dangerous, but we are still able to take some immediate, assertive action to prevent further problems.

On the fourth tab write, "When you feel things in your life are breaking down"

Then make a list of the warning signs which, **for you**, mean that things have worsened and are close to the crisis stage

Breaking down warning signs

Feeling needy

Racing or negative thoughts

In bed all the time or not sleeping well

Cannot concentrate

Cannot make decisions

Fractured thoughts jumping from subject to subject

Thoughts of worthlessness

Thoughts of suicide/thoughts of harming others

Seeing or hearing things

Delusions

Paranoia

Unable to feel any emotions

Cannot listen or engage in conversation

Over-spending

Not eating or eating too much

Substance abuse

Five minutes seems like an hour

An hour seems like five minutes

Dissociation

Taking risks and courting danger

Angry, frustrated

Not wanting to going to school or work

Control

Are you in control? You are somewhat; you are trying to hang in there!

It's worth having a plan and trying to break your fall!

On the next page, write an Growth Plan to use "When things are breaking down" include things you think will help reduce the situation when they have progressed to this point

The plan now needs to be very directive with fewer choices and very clear instructions

Can you alter this daily plan mid-stream? Judgment and analysis skills may be poor, so answer clearly. How can you stay in control?

Breaking down plan "Must Do's"

<u>Symptoms</u>	<u>Action</u>
In bed all the time	Get out of bed
Crying at work	Take a long break outside or excuse yourself and ask to go home.
Feeling worthlessness	Read affirmations and meet with a family member or supporter
Can't concentrate	Do intense exercise at the gym on favorite machine for aerobics
Courting danger	Become safe—NO guns, pills, car keys, or credit cards.
Any severe symptoms	Carry out a Daily Growth Plan

Development Plan

The next section of your LIFE CHANGING SELF AWARENESS is the Development Plan.

In spite of your best planning and assertive action, you may find yourself in a **bad situation** where others will need to assist you. These situations may feel as though you are totally out of control.

Write Development Plan when things in your life are going well

Write a Development Plan when things in your life are going well, to instruct others about how to assist you.

It keeps you in **control** even when it seems like things are out of control. Others will know what to do, saving everyone time and frustration, while ensuring that **your** needs are met.

On the fifth tab, write "Development Plan" and insert quite a few sheets of lined paper because the Development Plan has (9) parts.

Part (1) When life is going great

Describe what you are like when things in your life are going great. You can copy this from the first part of the Daily Growth Plan
"What I'm like when things in my life are going well"

An example of you descriptive words might be:

Talkative	Quiet	Outgoing	Withdrawn
Adventurous	Cautious	Outspoken	Reserved
Ambitious	Laid back	Retiring	Intellectual
Humorous	Sensible	Practical	Energetic
Funny	Calm	Well-groomed	Dressed nicely
Happy			

Part (2) Warning Signs

Clearly describe those warning signs that would indicate to others that they need to assist you with your care and make decisions on your behalf.

The symptoms might include:

➢ Uncontrollable pacing, unable to stay still

➢ Severely agitated depression

➢ Inability to stop compulsive behaviors

➢ Catatonic and unmoving for long periods of time

➢ Neglecting personal hygiene (for 3 days or longer)

➢ Extreme mood swings daily

➢ Destructive to property

➢ Not understanding what people are saying

➢ Self-destructive behavior

➢ Abusive or violent behavior-dangerous to self or others

➢ Criminal activities

➢ Substance abuse

➢ Threatening suicide—or acting suicidal

➢ Not getting out of bed at all for 2 days

➢ Refusing to eat or drink for 2 days

Part (3) Supporters/Support Channel

List at least 5 people you can depend on when warning signs you have listed come up. This includes family members, friends and/or education professionals. The following are examples of attributes you may want from those who take over and make decisions for you:

Responsible	Honest	Sincere
Knowledgeable	Calm	Compassionate
Understanding	Trustworthy	

Include, if desired:

"I do not want the following people in any way involved in assisting me with any matter:
Name: _____
Why you do not want then involved (optional)
Settling disputes between supporters—include a section that describes how you want disputes between supporters settled.

Part (4) Medications

➢ List the name and phone numbers of your physician and pharmacy

➢ List your allergies

➢ List the medications including OTC meds you are currently using and why you are taking them

➢ List those medications you would accept to take if medications (or additional medications) become necessary and why you would prefer them

➢ List those medications that should be avoided and give reasons for unacceptability

Part (5) Respite Care

➢ Develop a plan so that you can stay at home or in the community and still get the care you need.

Part (6) Treatment Facilities

➢ List those treatment facilities where you would prefer to be hospitalized if that becomes necessary and list those you wish to avoid.

Part (7) Help from others

➢ Write "What I need my supporters to do for me that would help reduce warning signs/symptoms which caused the unhealthy situation"

   o   Give me the space to express my feelings

   o   Don't talk to me—or do talk to me

   o   Encourage me and reassure me

   o   Feed me good food

   o   Make sure I get exposure to outdoor light for at least 30 minutes daily.

   o   Keep me from hurting myself, or others even if that means you have to restrain me or get help from others.

   o   Listen to me without giving me advice, judging me or criticizing me.

   o   Hold me

   o   Let me pace

   o   Encourage me to move

   o   Lead me through a relaxation or stress-reduction exercise.

   o   Peer counsel with me

   o   Take me for a walk

   o   Provide me with materials so I can draw, write or paint, etc.

Part (8) Do Not's from others

- ➢ Force me to do anything
- ➢ Play certain kinds of music (which kinds?)
- ➢ Play certain videos (what sort?)
- ➢ Be impatient with me
- ➢ Make me feel ignored
- ➢ Try to entertain me
- ➢ Chatter
- ➢ Get angry with me
- ➢ Make me feel invalid

Part (9) Work from others

- ➢ At the top of another page write "what I need others to do for me".
- ➢ Make a list of things you need others to do for you and who you want to do what.
- ➢ It might include paying bills, talking to doctors, or caring for individuals.

Things will get better soon!!

Your supporters will know by some of the following:

- ➢ When I have slept through the night for three nights
- ➢ When I begin cooking for myself
- ➢ When I eat at least two good meals a day
- ➢ When I am taking care of my personal hygiene needs
- ➢ When I carry on a conversation
- ➢ When I keep my living space organized, clean
- ➢ When I can be in a crowd without being anxious
- ➢ When I can return to work
- ➢ When I can sit still for 10 minutes

(Note that these are only examples—you will have your own signs of survival)

Pre-Development Plan

➢ You are getting better

➢ You are fragile

➢ You need support

➢ Your Achievement Tools are the same

➢ Perhaps you may have new fears and anxieties

Life Challenges

➢ Carrying on a conversation

➢ Standing in a line

➢ Grocery shopping

➢ Mingling

➢ Introducing yourself to someone

➢ Challenging someone about something

➢ Doing something without being asked

➢ Asking for something; a job, date, etc.

➢ Feeling that you'll never be able to work again

➢ Getting gas

➢ Asserting a need that you have

➢ Feeling that you are being watched

➢ Fearing someone dislikes you

➢ Isolating yourself

➢ Taking advantage of care and pity

➢ Wondering if medications are working right

➢ Settling for less than you deserve

➢ Having trouble repelling stigma

Pre-Development Plan

Challenge	Action to Take
Isolating	Be around people
Settling for less	Do only what is in your best interest. It's no more than you deserve.
Not doing your share	Do your share unasked
Feeling watched or disliked	Think of affirmations or start a conversation
Feeling stigma	Study affirmations
Having negative thoughts	Use cognitive therapy
Getting too much care	Doing more for yourself
Asking for a date or job	Take time and visualize success—if you don't succeed, that's okay, you tried.
Feeling unorganized	Follow LIFE CHANGING SELF AWARENESS Plans

Improving Life
Always do what is in your best interest!!

➢ Monitor your pace of activity

➢ Examine your living space and environment

➢ Examine your lifestyle

➢ How can you enhance your life?

➢ What do you want to do?

Pace of Activity

If you are starting to isolate and slow down in your interactions with others—then plan some activities that involve interaction with others that stimulate you.

If your life is moving too fast, with too many things going on, slow things down by taking some time for yourself. Maybe planning a low-key activity such as reading, renting a video or just watching TV.

Be aware of your physical and mental limits—and set your boundaries accordingly.

Living Space/Environment

➤ Do you look forward to going home?

➤ Is your home safe and secure?

➤ Is your home uncluttered, attractive and comfortable?

➤ Do you have private space in your home that is respected by others?

➤ If you live with others, do they enhance your wellness?

➤ Is your home easily accessible to needed services?

➤ Is your home easy to maintain?

➤ Do you need to make some changes in your living situations?

Lifestyle

➤ Is your lifestyle too hectic and chaotic?

➤ Are you always taking care of others and not taking care of yourself?

➤ Do you try to do too much everyday?

➤ Do you take on more than you should?

➤ Do you have more things than you need?

➤ Do all these things make your life difficult to manage?

➤ Are there people in your life that make your life chaotic

➤ Do you need to make some lifestyle changes?

Enhancing your Life

➤ What could you do to enhance the quality of your life?

➤ Would a pet help?

➤ How does color affect the way you feel? What changes could you make to increase your exposure to colors that would make you feel better?

➤ Is there anyway you could use music to enhance your life?

➤ How does water make you feel? If it helps, could you increase your exposure to water?

What do you want to do?

You will become happy, build growth and independence!

Do you have a job to return to?

➢ Do you like it?

➢ Does your employer understand?

➢ Do you need a change?

What do you like to do? What makes you happy?

Is there a certain job or career direction you have?

What kind of a job might you like?

➢ Would you like to work full or part-time?

➢ Would you like to work for someone else? Or yourself?

Could you create your own job?

For the job you want-

➢ What preparation and planning might be needed?

➢ What education and training would be needed?

Working can be very satisfying and fulfilling—but only if it's the right job for you!

Taking care of yourself—As you move forward

1. Feeling Hope & Dreams and unaffected by stigma

2. Taking self responsibility for our illness

3. Being a strong self-advocate

4. Continuing self-education

5. Having a strong support system

6. Monitoring and improving thoughts & improving self-esteem

7. Using and adding to our affirmations

8. Knowing and using your Achievement Tools

9. Creating, following and updating your plans

10. Using medication and therapy as needed

11. Avoiding vulnerabilities

12. Enjoying your sense of humor

13. Having a safe, comfortable living environment

14. Having financial stability

15. Doing thing you like to do

16. Having a good time

17. Balance lifestyle

18. Building a harmonious family life

19. Loving yourself (others will follow)

20. Seeing, helping, caring for and loving others

21. Staying on top of your illness!!

22. Enjoying your life!!

Authors Bio

Kelvin Batten devotes his time exploring new frontiers of Personal and Career Development Education, especially as it relates to showing people from all walks of life what they can do by themselves for themselves to achieve their set goals in life and/or at work, despite the limitations of their circumstances or environment. To play this role effectively, Kelvin using himself as a "guinea pig" of sorts to explore, discover and document best practice ways of successfully venturing into various areas of endeavor.

In a previous life, Kelvin further held numerous executive positions with fortune 500 companies, during which time he successfully employed personal growth and professional development techniques to give himself a consistent edge as Director, and later Training and Development Vice President. For instance, he built a reputation for using self-taught spreadsheet programming skills in his spare time to develop Automated Spreadsheet Applications to computerize manual report generation processes in the departments he worked. Over four (4) of his applications were formally adopted for executive level reporting. This was in addition to constantly challenging the status quo and influencing positive work changes.

Before voluntarily resigning from his executive position (to pursue a long standing dream of running his own business), he successfully held Senior Management and Executive Management roles as Director of Operations and later Vice President of Operations. Kelvin presently support and serve with professional networking a group, including joining the Executive Networking Who's Who, The Oklahoma Mental Health Consumer Council, Tulsa Oklahoma's Toastmaster Professionals, Local Advocate groups for Individuals Personal and Career Development, Developmental Disabilities and Behavioral Health. Additionally, he is a member of The Tulsa Oklahoma Chamber of Commerce and held various positions with the Hampton Roads Chamber of Commerce.

I have always loved writing and speaking, especially about application of one's personal knowledge and experiences towards achieving set goals and objectives in life (i.e. via Self-Development).

My objective while giving talks on personal growth and professional development, is to influence the mental attitude of my audience so they adopt ways of thinking that will enable them achieve significant and consistent improvements in their personal and workplace performances.

"It is my vision that through the work I now do, and by sharing a lot of my significant achievements in education, paid employment, personal experiences and growth, with those who express interest, I will help others aspire to, and achieve their fullest possible potentials in life. I intend to equip myself to do this by learning from my experiences, studying what others have done and reaching out to those who have gone ahead of me and who indicate willingness to help for assistance".

—Kelvin Batten

Jeffrey A. Brown personally integrates his passion for understanding universal truths (and inspiring others to do the same) with his passion for creating positive changes in the world.

As a young entrepreneur, Jeffrey embarked on his mission to discover what he is in this world to do, at the same time understanding his mission in life is pretty simple, to change the world by inspiring and empowering people to live at their highest potential while using their strengths in the greatest service to the world.

In a previous life, He further held numerous senior management and executive positions with fortune 500 companies, during which time he successfully created educational resources for youth and adult audiences to aid in their pursuit of personal growth and professional development. Jeffrey is particularly fond of gathering and crafting stories that teach, transform and inspire others. With irreverent humor and an innate sense of the absurd, Jeff's talks and writings help people see how needlessly complex and stressful our lives can become. He has also delivered career and personal counseling to hundreds of individuals as a professional career counselor.

Throughout his career, Jeffrey has often found that people with strong spiritual underpinnings are more successful in their business and personal lives. What's more, he has observed a large spiritual component separating the true inspirational leader from the mere manager. He came to see the Bible, the major inspirational treatise for the majority of America's citizens, as a wellspring of leadership wisdom and inspiring "case studies" for modern business.

Before voluntarily resigning from his executive position (to pursue a long standing dream of running his own business), he successfully held Senior Management and Executive Management roles as Manager of Operations and Vice President of Smarter Solutions. He presently supports and serves with professional networking groups, such as The Tulsa Oklahoma Chamber of Commerce, The Oklahoma Mental Health Consumer Council, Tulsa Young Professionals, Tulsa Oklahoma's Toastmaster Professionals, Local Advocate groups for Individuals Personal Growth and Professional Development, Developmental Disabilities and Behavioral Health, as well as a Service Provider for the State of Oklahoma's Department of Rehabilitation Services and Department of Human Services Developmental Disabilities Service Division.

"Success means something different for everyone. For me, it is turning an idea into reality—it means taking the things I love—and translating that into a profitable business. By applying the key principles and concepts provided in this book, has given me the ability to overcome resistance and move forward in achieving all that I can dream-taking nothing and turning into something!"

—**Jeffrey A. Brown**

978-0-595-47756-2
0-595-47756-9

www.ingramcontent.com/pod-product-compliance
Lightning Source LLC
Chambersburg PA
CBHW020420290526
45785CB00002B/654